# GABRIEL FAURÉ

Charles Koechlin

# GABRIEL FAURÉ

( 1845 - 1924 )

DENNIS DOBSON LIMITED

MCM  XLVI

FIRST PUBLISHED IN GREAT BRITAIN IN 1946 BY

DENNIS DOBSON LIMITED
29 GREAT QUEEN STREET
KINGSWAY, LONDON, W.C.2

Second Edition (revised)

TRANSLATED FROM THE FRENCH BY LESLIE ORREY

PRINTED IN GREAT BRITAIN
*in 10pt. Times*
BY THE PORTSDOWN PRESS, LTD.
FLEET LANE, LONDON, E.C.4

# CONTENTS

# Introduction

There are signs in this country that Gabriel Fauré is at last about to receive some of the recognition due to him, and there must be many, both among his old admirers and among those who are only just beginning to savour the distinctive delights of his style, who will be eager to supplement the somewhat meagre biographical details given in Grove and other reference books. This, the first Life of Fauré to appear in English, will, I hope, go some way towards satisfying this demand.

There are, indeed, several reasons why Koechlin's monograph should find a welcome among English readers. In the first place, it is of value not only for the biographical details of Fauré's life, but for its discussion of practically the whole of his output,—which, although not vast, will no doubt appear surprisingly large and varied to all but the few who know his work intimately.

Secondly, the unstinted praise which Koechlin lavishes on his former teacher, supported by the numerous quotations from such distinguished French musicians as Mme. Nadia Boulanger and M. Emil Vuillermoz, Roger-Ducasse and Cortot, and reinforced by the considerable bibliography which he appends, is an index of the esteem in which Fauré is held in his native land. This esteem, it should be noted, is not confined to a narrow circle of the intelligentsia ; and for proof of this one has but to turn to the lengthy list of his music which, from time to time, has been made available on gramophone records. The catalogue in " The Gramophone Shop Encyclopedia " (New York, 1936), extends to over 60 works, including the String Quartet, the C minor Piano Quartet, the 1st Violin Sonata, the Requiem (complete), and the song cycles *la Bonne Chanson* and *l'Horizon chimérique*—and this does not, of course, include the important recordings recently made of the Theme and Variations, and other works. It would be idle to expect the general public to endorse this opinion in its entirety, and indeed Koechlin himself confesses that Fauré's music is not for the multitude. Nevertheless there can be no doubt that the circle of his friends is widening, and that more and more English musicians are yielding to the spell of this " supremely civilised music."

Finally, the book offers an admirable illustration of the temper of French criticism in the 1920's. Koechlin himself (born 1867) is distinguished as both composer and critic, though few of his works are known over here ; and what he has to say, no less than his manner of saying it, is of interest to every student of modern French music.

The list of works, taken without alteration from Koechlin's original, which in turn was founded on that in *la Revue musicale* of October 1922, is not quite complete. (1) Léon Vallas, in his " Claude Debussy : his life and works," mentions (p. 44 of the English translation) a " Passion," rehearsed at one of the *Société nationale* concerts, in 1890,

vii

which I have not been able to trace. (2) the catalogue in the Gramophone Shop Encyclopedia includes a recording (withdrawn), of a Noel, " Il est né, le divin enfant," written when Fauré was at the Madeleine, but never published (recorded by Pathé). (3) Jankélévitch mentions an "*Aurore*," still in manuscript, in the library of the Paris Conservatoire. (4) There is also " *Mélisande's Song*," to English words, written for the London production. (5) The second String Quartet which " Grove " mentions is certainly non-existent ; the Quartet, Op. 121, was Fauré's only essay in this form.

I have not thought it necessary to include, in the Bibliography, a list of some two dozen articles from various French journals ; instead I have added a few French books not included in Koechlin's list, and also appended a short list of books and articles in English. For the rest, I have left Koechlin's book as he wrote it, merely providing a few notes here and there, and adding an Index.

My thanks are due to many friends in Cambridge for their interest and help, with a particular debt of gratitude to Mrs. David Thomson ; also to the Professor of Music and the University Library Authorities, for permission to consult books and scores in the Pendlebury and University Libraries ; and to the proprietors of *la Revue musicale*, for permission to reproduce the fine drawing from the issue of October, 1922. The picture used as frontispiece is due to the kind offices of Mr. Felix Aprahamian, to whom I tender my sincere thanks for his interest and help. Finally, I cannot say how much I owe to the courtesy and patience of Mr. Dobson ; his help and advice through all stages of the book's progress have been invaluable.

LESLIE ORREY

*Cambridge, May,* 1945.

# Biographical

GABRIEL-URBAIN FAURÉ was born on 12th May, 1845, at Pamiers, a little town in the Ariège District, in the South of France near the Pyrennees. His forbears,[1] so A. Bruneau tells us, were " active traders contributing prosaically but usefully to the nourishment of their fellow-citizens "—or, in less flowery language, butchers. His father, a teacher at Gaillac-Toulza, married Mademoiselle de Laleine-Laprade, daughter of a retired captain—beautiful, but poor. The couple, by no means in easy circumstances but highly cultivated, had six children ; Gabriel was the last. His birthplace was in Rue Major, near the market place. Baptised in the Church of Notre-Dame du Camp, his infancy was spent with foster-parents in nearby Verniolles, until his father (then sub-Inspector of elementary education) was appointed Director of l'École Normale at Montgauzy, not far from Foix. The little Gabriel was by then four years old, and returned to the family circle. This École Normale was located in an old, disestablished convent, whose Chapel, however, still functioned. The child had no greater joy than to go there and listen to the modest harmonium, which was his introduction to music. All the splendours of the mountains, too, were before his eyes, for the Chapel, as well as the Chateau de Foix, overlooked the wonderful Barguillière valley. As Bruneau says, " Nature generously yielded her secret to this simple child, a secret he could never forget ; she initiated him into the intimate lyricism of the Universe."

The harmonium tempted Gabriel. He would give free rein to his fancy, improvising at the instrument. It happened quite by chance that he had for audience one day a lady, elderly, blind, and also an excellent musician. Struck by his talents, she suggested to the parents that he should be sent to l'École Niedermeyer, a school which enjoyed a great and justifiable reputation. It appears that M. Fauré *père* was not slow in raising a number of objections ; like so many others, understanding nothing of the art of music, he regarded it merely as an agreeable pastime.[2] Nevertheless, he wrote to the Director. The fortunate coincidence of a concert tour bringing him as far as Foix allowed the composer of " *Le Lac* "[3] to verify these exceptional gifts. The young musician's future appeared so bright that, seeing the difficulties of the household, he took upon himself the expenses of his education—a fine generosity which smoothed away all obstacles.

L'École Niedermeyer, then as now, was a boarding establishment where the teaching of music was supplemented by tuition in general subjects. It was located in Rue Fontaine Saint-Georges (now Rue

---

[1]*Grandfather and great-grandfather.—Particulars from an Address given to the Institute by the composer of* Messidor.

[2]*Cf. l'Indépendance musicale et dramatique, September-October,* 1887 (*H. Imbert, Profils de musiciens : Gabriel Fauré*).

[3]" Le Lac," *song by Niedermeyer to words by Lamartine which achieved a considerable popularity.* (*Tr.*)

1

# Gabriel Fauré

Fromentin), not far from the " Remparts de Clichy." The bareness of his small bedroom, a state of things customary at the time, did not seem hard to the boy, now nine years old (1854). The main thing was the seriousness of his class studies, and the strict discipline which these entailed ; but on the other hand the opportunity of isolating his mind was never denied him, he was able to withdraw into himself without being engrossed by a thousand mundane distractions. All his life he treasured the memory of this schooling, somewhat austere no doubt but most valuable to him.

The study of Gregorian Modes figured in the curriculum of the school. It is impossible to attach too much importance to this, and we shall return to it later. Niedermeyer, if one can trust his pupil, was an educationist of the front rank. He died in 1861, and Harmony was thereafter taught by L. Dietsch, Maître de Chapelle at the Madeleine, and Conductor at l'Opéra : " by nature frigid, methodical but reactionary in mind." Fortunately, Fauré was admitted to the piano class, where he had as teacher Camille Saint-Saëns. And more than once in the course of time Fauré has proclaimed that he owed *everything* to this master. For Saint-Saëns did not restrict his role to that of a professor of piano—however scrupulous and exacting ; he opened the door to the whole of music. Bach first, with the 48 ; and then, the class over, he sat himself down to play Schumann, Liszt, even Wagner. Bear in mind that at this time such modernists were known only to rare initiates, those imbued by the modern spirit.[1] And remembering that Massenet was rejected by Bazin[2] as *too free*, one realises the distance separating the teaching at the Conservatoire from that which Gabriel Fauré received. Moreover, the master was eager to know the works of his pupils : " he read them with as much curiosity and care as if they were all masterpieces."[3]

The value of this education, complete, manysided, broad, and, with its balance between discipline and independence, encouraging the development of the boy's talent, is seen in the songs composed between 1865 and 1870, so novel for an epoch in which Adolphe Adam, Victor Massé, Halévy and Meyerbeer still flourished. On Sundays, with his inseparable Eugène Gigout, he would go off to the hill of Montmartre, at that time in open country. And, according to Bruneau, the sight of the monuments of Paris inspired in both of them definite and precise ambitions.—" I shall have the Madeleine," said Fauré—" And I, Saint-Augustin," replied Gigout. This was the highest and most wholesome ambition possible ; a hard way of life, poorly paid, but how profitable to the young musicians ! The atmosphere, religious, serious and noble (despite sometimes a lack of understanding on the part of the faithful, or even of the clergy) and the thousand resources which the organ offers for improvisation, led Fauré, like Franck, to the summits of musical art ; and, in that

---

[1] *And Saint-Saëns was one of them ; see his* Harmonie et Mélodie.

[2] *Bazin (1816-78), Professor of Harmony, later of Composition, at the Conservatoire. (Tr.)*

[3] *Cf. article by Fauré on Saint-Saëns in* la Revue Musicale, *February, 1922.*

2

extreme modesty which characterised him to the end of his days, almost without him suspecting it.

With the first prize for piano, organ, harmony and composition, he left l'École Niedermeyer and went off to Rennes some months later (January, 1866) in the capacity of organist of Saint-Sauveur's. He had already written, in 1865, *le Cantique de Racine*, a work whose Mendelssohnian style serves an inspiration delicate and profound, quite " Racinian "—more personal than one realises on first hearing. Other works, less successful (as for example *le Papillon et la Fleur*[1]), were not without some renown, whereas a song more decidedly Faurian would doubtless at that time not have been understood. Also, despite his surroundings and their influence on his technique, there was nothing of the ascetic about him. It is not, I think, that he led a very frivolous life. But the *curé* had to reproach him for smoking cigarettes in the church porch during the sermons. A more outrageous prank caused great scandal ; having spent the night at a ball at the Prefecture, he appeared at his organ seat in black coat and white tie. This was beyond all bounds, and he was dismissed. *Felix culpa*, for on returning to Paris, appointed to Notre-Dame de Clignancourt (1870) he renewed his acquaintanceship with Saint-Saëns and threw himself eagerly into the musical life of the city. Between 1865 and 1870, what had he composed? The first set of songs is by some ascribed to this period,[2] but other authorities (e.g., the collection of L. Cellier) suggest no more than one Prelude and Fugue. Which are we to choose between these two extremes ? The second assumption seems hardly credible, and we incline to the other.

In the month of August, 1870, war broke out, and Fauré enlisted in a regiment of *voltigeurs*. He was under fire at Champigny, and fought courageously. He heard of the armistice while on a mission as liaison officer, and, evading enlistment in the army of the Commune, he crossed the federal lines by the aid of a false passport, reaching Rambouillet where he awaited the victory of the Versailles armies. Soon afterwards we find him at the organ of Saint-Honoré d'Eylau ; later (still continuing to deputise for Saint-Saëns at the Madeleine), he assisted his friend Widor at Saint-Sulpice, and about the same time he re-entered l'École Niedermeyer—this time as Professor, with André Messager as his first pupil. On the resignation of Saint-Saëns in 1877 Fauré became Maître de Chapelle at the Madeleine in place of Dubois, promoted to organist. The same year he journeyed to Weimar with his master and friend for the *première* of Samson and Delilah under Liszt, at the theatre of the Grand Duke. He heard Valkyrie and Rhinegold at Cologne in 1878, and the complete tetralogy at Munich in 1879.

His duties in connection with the Church left him with time not only for his own work but for cultivating new friends. However, no one was less pushful than he. But his musical talents, above all his agreeable nature, procured him some useful acquaintances. Some

---

[1] *This youthful trifle was sung at Rennes by Mme. Miolan-Carvalho.*

[2] *Cf. the chronological list of Fauré's compositions in* la Revue Musicale ; *the date indicated for all these compositions is "about 1865."*

# Gabriel Fauré

were among his brother professionals ; but the most numerous, and perhaps the most convinced of his merit, were among cultivated, intelligent people, who could sometimes discern something of the magnitude of his future.

The Viardot family welcomed him with open arms. He himself loved this *salon*, animated by the rough vigour of the Slav Turgeneff. And then, he was not insensible to the beauty of Mlle. Marianne. The betrothal was decided ; but Pauline Viardot, above everything, loved the stage, and she did not hesitate to make known this taste to her future son-in-law, counting on his whole-hearted devotion to it also. However, incredible as it will appear to those who see in Fauré only an " *indolent charmeur*," the young artist, faithful to the profound intimacy of chamber music and song, refused to adopt a way of life he did not think his own,[1] and, despite extreme sorrow, he broke with the Viardots. Here is a rare example of conscience and hidden energy ; the inner strength of the master is only too often misunderstood, and it is a pleasure to point out this example of his will-power.

The period under review is moreover one of the most active and fruitful of a lifetime consecrated to work—labour exclusively centred on composition, had not the difficulties of making a living driven him to other tasks—as, in due course, that of Professor, and later Director of that august institution the Paris Conservatoire. From these years of his hard-working youth date the last songs of the first set and many of the second (*Nell, Automne*, etc.). The first Violin Sonata (1875) was played in 1878 at the Universal Exhibition,[2] and was published by Breitkopf and Härtel ; no French firm would undertake it. Fauré here has definitely found himself. But he had still to encounter many obstacles. The publication and performance of such works did not get any easier. It takes so little in the art of music to disconcert people ! Not that his harmony was unprecedented; but, written in an unfamiliar idiom and serving for the expression of new feelings, this music could not fail, very often, to be misunderstood.[3]

Naturally, publishers still welcomed him but coldly, and only Hamelle risked the venture. The risk at this time was small ; and, besides, each song was bought for an average of 50 francs (with no further rights on the sale). With the hard-headedness of the peasant " *père* Hamelle " proved sharper than his fellows ; and if he scarcely

---

[1] *At least at that time, since* Pénélope *was written much later, when he was past sixty.*

[2] *The performers were the violinist Maurin, with the composer at the piano. In 1877 Saint-Saëns wrote an enthusiastic article about this Sonata.*

[3] *We must make amends to Franz Liszt by correcting an error in the first edition, for which Bruneau's address to the Institute was responsible. In actual fact Liszt had perfectly well understood the Ballade that the young Fauré had brought him. But Fauré, overcome with nervousness, was unable to play a note ; Liszt then, full of understanding and sympathy both for his young confrère and the work (the value of which he appreciated fully), sat down at the piano to play it himself. And if, when it came to the Allegro, he had to stop, with the words (as has so often been related) ' it is too difficult ', the cause was certainly not lack of comprehension nor boredom, but simply because the old man's fingers refused to do his bidding.*

filled the musician's pocket the latter, nevertheless, owed to him the chance of having his works spread abroad, a difficult task while they were still in manuscript. The Violin Sonata had slipped through his hands, but he had his revenge with the first Quartet, acquired without loosening his purse-strings ;[1] indeed, with no expense beyond the engraving and printing. Added to this he had obtained, gratuitously, the rights in the profitable *Berceuse*. But such is the destiny of pioneers. Lalo, Franck, Debussy experienced similar difficulties, and no doubt it would be the same to-day for any composer of originality who took no advantage of the notoriety which a newcomer can always claim among snobs, and by which the publishers in their turn are influenced.

Happily, other support was forthcoming, and not only from among the musicians themselves.[2] Less perhaps from his marriage, in 1883, to Mlle. Marie Frémiet, the daughter of the well-known sculptor,[3] than from other acquaintances. Madame Fauré was essentially a woman of the home, a faithful wife and devoted mother of her family, absorbed in the care of her children ; her fine appearance is not easily forgotten.[4] But, attached as she was to her husband, and eager to see him appreciated at his true worth, she could do little to add to his renown. Fauré was forced to lead a life less homely than his family—not from choice, for he was not one of those flippant dilettantes for whom music is no more than a diversion—but in order to hear and help forward his works.

The dedications of some of his songs show us that they were welcomed by many of the fashionable singers : Mme. Henriette Escalier (afterwards Mme. Alexander Dumas), Mme. Baugnies (to-day, Mme. de Saint-Marceaux), Mme. Dettelbach (*Arpège*), Mme. Sigismond Bardac (now Mme. Claude Debussy), who, it is said, proved a wise counsellor, and was the faithful interpreter of the admirable *Bonne Chanson* which is dedicated to her.

You must bear in mind that this was the time when the composer of *Mignon* held Fauré to be a dangerous revolutionary. The latter would have liked one of the composition classes at the Conservatoire. The high official was indignant. Who did this intruder think he was ? He was not *Prix de Rome*, was not even from the workshop which produced them. " Fauré, never ! If he is nominated, I resign." This *veto* is authentic, confirmed by reliable witnesses.

Such ostracism need not astonish us. But the important thing is that this " dangerous revolutionary " had proved himself a true classic, and at the time of the refusal offered by the illustrious Thomas no serious artist worthy of the name could ignore the masterly technique which the Violin Sonata or the first Quartet already proclaimed. As

---

[1]*He drove the same bargain for the second Quartet.*

[2]*We shall deal later with the* Société Nationale.

[3]*However, Frémiet's help was precious when his son-in-law stood as candidate for the Institute ; it had already been useful in support of his composition pupils in the Rome competition. Fauré was not on the Board of Examiners since the Institute had not yet opened its doors to him.*

[4]*She died in 1925, scarcely a year after her husband.*

# Gabriel Fauré

for the simple " *mélodies*," *Clair de lune* suffices to reveal the great musician.

In compensation, supported by the *salons* of intelligent people, interpreted by excellent singers (Thérèse Roger, Jeanne Remacle, Mlle. Fanny Lépine, then[1] Mme. J. Raunay, Mme. J. Bathori, Mlle. Germaine Sanderson, Mme. Croiza, etc.), Fauré saw himself understood, little by little, by some composers of his generation—and above all by the younger men. The *Société Nationale* had been founded in 1871 and, as everybody knows, it has rendered great service to symphonic art in France. Although it breathed sometimes a spirit too exclusively Franckist (particularly after the death of Franck, for disciples always overrate their master), it welcomed personalities other than those disciples ; moreover, even among those, there were many who were just in their attitude towards Fauré—notably that broadminded and sincere artist, H. Duparc.

The *Nationale* was of great help to him ; he never tired of acknowledging the debt and took care, right to the end, to reserve for it the greater part of his first performances. It was the *Nationale* which first presented the two Piano Quartets ; numerous and beautiful songs ; *Nocturnes ; Barcarolles.* They were evenings of rare charm, as were the concerts when later, between 1890 and 1900, the music of Chabrier and Debussy came to console us with many a ray of light in the prevailing darkness. On the other hand, the *Requiem* (1888) was performed at the Madeleine where Fauré, as has been said, was Maître de Chapelle.[2] The symphonic style tempted him less (and besides, he accorded only secondary importance to the art of instrumentation). A Violin Concerto, a Suite for Orchestra and a Symphony in D Minor remain unpublished. Ever exacting where his own work was concerned, the composer judged these vast compositions to be too uneven and, who knows ? perhaps too ambitious.

Finally, for the Odéon he wrote : in 1888, the incidental music to Alexander Dumas' *Caligula*, and in 1889 that to *Shylock* (adapted from Shakespeare by E. Haraucourt). The second set of songs was almost finished ; after the second Piano Quartet (1886), these fruitful years saw the birth of *les Présents, Clair de lune, Nocturne, Larmes, au Cimetière, Spleen.* And the collection " *de Venise* "[3] put the seal on his reputation as an interpreter of Verlaine, apart from that unique episode in his career, *la Bonne Chanson.* With *Soir, Arpège* and the beautiful duet *Pleurs d'or*, he turned to Albert Samain. At about the same time, too, he finished the charming four-handed Suite, *Dolly*, and the delightful sixth Nocturne.

We must not look for " grand adventures " in this career, so modest and industrious, where society gatherings were only a custom necessary

---

[1]*This is to anticipate ; the names which follow belong to a more recent epoch, bringing us to our own times.*

[2]*Then, in 1900, at the Universal Exhibition.*

[3]*It was in 1890, thanks to the generosity of Mme. la princesse de Polignac, that Fauré became acquainted with Venice. It is extraordinary, but true, that his Barcarolle (from the first volume) so thoroughly Venetian, had been imagined ; but we have it from the master himself that he has been only twice in the city of the Doges : when he composed the six songs and, more recently, a few years before his death.*

for the production of his music, and concerts and evenings at the theatre only professional engagements. But his life was not entirely taken up with breadwinning ; there were happy leisure hours consecrated to this monument of great musical culture, witness of an epoch of enthusiasm, individualism, and—in the widest sense—of faith. His fame now was growing. One no longer dared to scoff at him as a dangerous iconoclast. The *Nationale* concerts, the sympathy of the *élite*, and this stream of works of the first order placed him at the head of our musicians for those who could discern true merit. I know that many brother musicians, many a critic and many amateurs who consider themselves knowledgeable in these matters can see in him nothing but a pleasant composer of little tunes. No matter ; each year sees the circle of his initiates widened, the work of that band of unknown but devoted friends who make the reputations of great artists and thrust them on posterity. This living power of beauty, once a certain extension of its influence has been achieved, becomes irresistible ; once it wins the true connoisseurs among the public—the men of goodwill—it is henceforward that gentle power, insistent and persuasive, which triumphs over all obstacles—even envy and slander. It is remarkable that Fauré, without intrigue, independent, individual, making concessions to nobody, nevertheless achieved a high official position at the Institute, with honours later showered upon him and an impressive funeral ceremony at his death.

He was over fifty (at that time, one did not " arrive " quickly) when his fame, against which prejudice and ignorance availed nothing, opened for him the doors of that Conservatoire from whence the preceding director, Thomas, had thought to exclude him. On his (Thomas's) death, Dubois had succeeded him. Massenet, who had canvassed for the post (and moreover would only accept on condition that he was elected for life), the illustrious and triumphal creator of *Manon*, checked for the first time in his life, sent in his resignation (from his composition class). It seemed that it would be difficult to replace this eminent teacher—without a peer, less even for the success of his pupils in the Rome competition than for the value of an education both traditional and liberal. Whom could one suggest ? Saint-Saëns, extraordinarily talented and confident, was of too restless a disposition to bind himself to so sedentary an occupation ; Paul Dukas was too young. Then Fauré offered himself (in 1897, the same year as *le Parfum Impérissable* was composed). The name of the minister who made the choice is unfortunately withheld from us ; he showed himself either a competent musician, or else very ably advised.

With Florent Schmitt, Louis Aubert, G. Enesco, Pierre Maurice, Mlle. J. Boulay, and R. Laparra, I was a pupil of Massenet ; with them I stayed for some years in Fauré's class. I already knew him, having met him at friends' houses (notably the lamented Jules Griset, whose choirs sang marvellously *le Ruisseau, les Djinns, Madrigal, Caligula*, the *Requiem* . . .). I liked his good-naturedness, his extreme simplicity. Somewhat distant now and then, rather from his introspective nature than from pride (nor even from indifference to the respect of his followers). But above all, I was drawn by his art, an attraction dating from the impression made upon me by the production at the Odéon of *Shylock*, with his exquisite incidental music. It will be imagined how happy I was to work under the direction of a musician whom I so profoundly admired.

In the presence of such a one we all felt both a little shy and immensely stimulated. A fine spirit pervaded his class ; already his personality made itself felt. If we imagine, in Fauré's place, some pretentious nobody, or some honest academic (as, for example, Lenepveu), would Ravel have been there, or Roger-Ducasse, or Paul Ladmirault ? It is very doubtful. But, like the needle to the magnet, they rallied to the new master.[1]

A distinguished member of the Conservatoire said recently to one of his friends : " One must not bore one's pupils ; perhaps it is better not to direct them too strictly. It is preferable that a professor should write beautiful music, and have, like Fauré, a fine appearance." This apparent paradox, pronounced by a man both methodical and clear-thinking, is borne out by the example of Fauré. A good appearance, certainly. One recalls, under the white hair, that Mediterranean face, bronzed, with his moustaches and Roman nose, and that aspect as of an Eastern dreamer, the eyes, dark-ringed, lost in strange milky luminosities of the pupil. But this, for us, was accessory ; the musician's *work* was the thing. And this work impelled us on.

After Massenet, whose volubility dispensed a teaching active, living, vibrant, and moreover comprehensive, Fauré seemed to read the works of his pupils in silence. In actual fact he did make some observations, rather rare, but useful in their sobriety, and always aimed at an improvement in style. For this " revolutionary " proved himself, as a teacher, to be a purist who detested clumsiness and carelessness. The most efficient spur, nevertheless, was that provided by himself, and the high standard of his own art ; his pupils offering to so true a musician only the very best they could write, and fearing, as unworthy of his artistic integrity, any concession or platitude. Certainly it would be a singular insensitiveness that would invite him to listen to anything banal or pompous. However, some did risk it : Fauré would then remain calm and quiet. He would become vacant, distant ; and, the audition over, would turn nonchalently, and ask softly, with an air of detachment, " Was there nothing else ? " All would understand—except the culprit, naturally incorrigible.

The influence of this Faurian music, both charming and profound, was excellent. A teaching more dogmatic or biassed would have been dangerous. If that of Fauré, far from scholasticism (though not from a strictness of writing, to which he held staunchly) was now and

---

[1]*Here, in alphabetical order, is a list of the more important pupils to pass through Fauré's class :    Louis Aubert, Mlle. Nadia Boulanger, Mlle. J. Boulay, Mlle. Campagna, E. Cools, Defosse, Roger Ducasse, G. Enesco, H. Estienne, G. Grovlez, H. Février, Mme. J. Herscher, Ch. Koechlin, P. Ladmirault, R. Laparra, Le Boucher, E. Malherbe, L. Masson, Pierre Maurice, Mazellier, Meunier, J. Morpain, M. Ravel, Florent Schmidt, E. Trémisot, E. Vuillermoz. As private pupil, outside the Conservatoire, M. François Berthet.*

then incomplete in certain details—e.g., orchestration—that mattered little ; besides, several of his pupils filled this gap by lessons with André Gedalge.[1] But after all, in spite of the fact that his method seemed so different, Fauré continued in his own way the work of Massenet, directing his pupils towards a musicianship based on a serious technique.[2]

The decision to accept this post was taken not entirely from motives of ambition, but more especially, it must be said, for its material advantages. It was impossible to live on what his composer's rights brought in, nor even on the sale of his compositions (we have specified the rates). His salary from the Conservatoire, 3,000 francs, was by no means a negligible sum, though deplorably reduced. To these resources, as well as some private lessons, had just been added his fees as organist at the Madeleine (he had succeeded Th. Dubois in 1896)—as Inspector of the provincial Conservatoires—and lastly, since 1903, as Music Critic of le Figaro. Happily, these diverse activities left him some free time. He could continue to write to please himself, and the years from 1896 to 1905 were still fairly fruitful. Many admirable songs (le Parfum impérissable, la Forêt de Septembre, etc.), a powerful work for piano (Thème et variations), other pieces of smaller dimensions, but which are far from negligible, the incidental music to Pelléas et Mélisande, and lastly that still too little known masterpiece, Prométhée—such, in spite of all his other ancillary occupations, is the record of this period of assiduous toil.

The Pelléas of Maeterlinck was to be given in London in 1898, at the Prince of Wales' Theatre ; Fauré composed some interludes, and went himself to conduct the orchestra. This music is well known ;[3] a Suite of extracts has been often performed. As it is now an open secret, especially since M. Vuillermoz has disclosed the fact in his contribution to " Fifty Years of French Music,"[4] I can confess that Fauré did me the honour to entrust the orchestration to me. He has admitted collaboration of this sort ; perhaps even the instrumental score of Pénélope is not entirely his work.

With regard to Prométhée, the performers were innumerable ; choirs, soloists, two wind bands (that of the Lyre Bitterroise, and that of a Regiment of Engineers, from Montpellier) supported by an imposing mass of strings and some fifteen harps. The scoring was the work of the Bandmaster of the Regiment, a difficult task, carried out in a manner which could not be bettered. It is well known that these performances at Béziers had, before the war (1914-18), been undertaken and subsidised by the sympathetic Bitterois patron, Castelbon de Beauxhostes.[5] It is owing to him that something

---

[1] And for Fugue too ; for example, Florent Schmitt, Maurice Ravel and the present writer.
[2] He had a horror for the Cantata of the Prix de Rome. In this competition his pupils succeeded less often than those of Massenet ; but this is not a point of importance. On the other hand, in his class chamber music benefited by a lively sympathy ; which there is no cause to regret.
[3] In France, that is ; it is less familiar over here. (Tr.)
[4] Published by la Librairie de France.
[5] At the instigation of his friend, Camille Saint-Saëns.

of the art of Greece has been revived. *Prométhée* will be discussed again at greater length in a following chapter. Its history can be dealt with in a few lines. The work was written in the winter and spring of 1900 ; the composer as he wrote it sent it off to his orchestrator, along with some general indications as to colour and *nuance*. Then he went to Béziers to undertake personally the final rehearsals. These were for him unforgettable days. He found himself again in his native southern country ; the hot sun gave to both things and people an intense life. The choristers worked, in the evenings, under the open sky, the dark blue infinity studded with great diamonds. The combined rehearsals took place in the Arena, in the brilliant glare of radiant afternoons. A general exultation communicated to all the performers the longing, the desire, to understand and to love. Those who have not seen it can have no conception of this bold and superb reproduction of the ancient tragedy.[1]

The case of Béziers is memorable, because an appeal was made to the ordinary citizens for the male portions of the chorus ; they proved once more that in this regard, amateurs are capable of excellent results. (The instrumentalists of *la Lyre Bitterroise* were doubtless not in the first class, nor as good technically as their *confrères* from Montpellier, but in the end they acquitted themselves most honourably in this difficult score, and the ensemble was magnificent.) We understand that other towns of the Midi, notably Narbonne, have followed this example. Some day perhaps we may be able to do things in the North with as much intelligence and zeal.

*Prométhée* is a landmark in the life of Gabriel Fauré—his first contact with Greek art.[2] It influenced the remainder of his career, and from then on his art tended towards a simplification almost to the point of bareness, reduced to essentials ; themes of a Doric purity and, in short, the resurrection of the spirit of Greece in a modern idiom (we shall return to this at greater length in the last chapter). Equally important is *la Forêt de Septembre* (1903), so heart-rending in its premonitions of the future. It seems that from this moment the musician, little by little, felt old age gaining on him. There is a singular gravity, occasionally indeed to be found in works anterior to this[3] but whose accent, here, takes on a decisive character, born of the composer's personal, living experience.

Certainly, he had kept his youth well. Youthful in gait, in intelligence and inspiration ; musically ever on the alert, his heart still tender, his body firm despite his age. At Béziers, approaching his sixtieth birthday, he leapt up the steps of the amphitheatre with ease. One had the impression that this little man—not, indeed, athletic, but by no means old—would continue the same for many years to come. And so in fact he appeared to us, right up to 1917 or 1918.

When Th. Dubois retired, in 1905, it was with some little astonish-

---

[1] *We were privileged to be present the following year. We have attempted to describe our impressions in an article in the* Revue Musicale, *on " The Theatre of Gabriel Fauré " (October, 1922).*

[2] *If we except* la Rose, *Hellenic certainly, but less powerful and naturally on smaller lines.* Caligula *and* Lydia *are* Roman ; *Fauré's instinct never failed him.*

[3] *Cf.* Thème et Variations, *and the 7th Nocturne, in C Sharp Minor.*

ment that I learnt that Fauré was succeeding him as Director of the Conservatoire. I had never imagined that he would have this official honour bestowed on him ; besides, I could not credit that he had accepted such engrossing duties ! But the news was true. Although almost torture to him, he was constrained to give up his time to administrative business, the greater part of which could as well have been transacted by any of his colleagues. Without a doubt, the minister offering him the post did him honour ; but he could have done without it. He was miserable at not being able to compose, and one can only deplore the strange way our Third Republic has of " supporting " its intellectuals. When a great musician like Gabriel Fauré, when an artist of exceptional worth—a national figure —has not the means necessary to existence, because fine music brings in almost nothing, because wealth is the monopoly of operettas, of the music-hall and the veristic drama[1]—when, for this artist, it is a question of providing for himself and his family, is it not a barbarous stupidity that he should be engulfed by lessons, or compelled to orchestrate I know not what, or again, reduced to receiving a thousand importunators, from morning till night, if he directs a Conservatoire ? Perhaps, if one could admit that the personality of the Director might create music and induce a healthy outlook in an establishment as vast as that of Paris, one would not have such lively regrets for the time lost by Fauré. But is this admissible ? It is probable, on the contrary, that he had more influence as a mere professor of composition. Once in the Director's chair he found himself estranged from his young pupils. However, he applied himself to certain reforms. In the singing classes the repertoire was enlarged—improved, where possible. More classics ; and *lieder* such as the Erl King and Margaret at the Spinning Wheel.[2] On the examination boards for Harmony, Counterpoint and Fugue appeared such notable musicians as Claude Debussy, Maurice Ravel, Paul Dukas. Naturally, the most gifted candidates had nothing to complain of. But after all these were small improvements, which others besides himself could have introduced ; whereas the direction of the Conservatoire took up all his time. It is remarkable that, despite so little leisure, the balance for the years 1905 to 1920 remains so favourable ;[3] three new

---

[1] With the exception of a few hallowed masterpieces, by chance become lucrative.

[2] In the instrumental classes it remained very difficult to modify the repertoire. The competition pieces stress, principally, virtuosity ; but this tradition is so powerful that it would require a " revolution " in the Conservatoire to accord to phrasing, style and rhythm the importance which belongs to them—as, on the other hand, to admit music other than that commonly known as classic ; I mean, to pay more heed to the 16th and 17th centuries, or to allow the existence of modern, even contemporary, classics. As for the composer's technique, one innovation is quite certainly attributable to Gabriel Fauré ; it is the counterpoint class. This has scarcely come up to expectations. It is clear that in the time of Massenet and Guiraud the majority of pupils wrote better fugues than they do to-day ; this was due to a number of causes and we have not the time to discuss them here. But particularly, it was quite illogical to separate counterpoint from fugue ; for administrative reasons, counterpoint should have been kept in the composition class. Since M. Rabaud's taking over the division has been different : 1st, counterpoint and fugue ; 2nd, musical composition. But we would prefer the combined instruction of Massenet, with A. Gedalge to help when needed on the purely technical side, when the master was otherwise engaged.

[3] In quality, if not in quantity ; for this period of fifteen years certainly shows a slackening off in production.

# Gabriel Fauré

volumes of songs (*la Chanson d'Ève*, *le Jardin clos*, *Mirages*), the first Quintet, *Pénélope* (Monte-Carlo, 4th May, 1913—then at the Champs-Elysées theatre, under G. Astruc), the second Violin Sonata, the first 'Cello Sonata, and the *Fantaisie* for Piano and Orchestra.

A double recognition rewarded him during these years of officialdom. In 1909 the Institute welcomed him ; 27 years after Paladilhe, 31 after Massenet—though these were almost his contemporaries : which makes one wonder concerning the choice of the illustrious company to which neither Rodin, nor Degas, nor Franck, nor Debussy ever belonged. And secondly the larger publishers began to notice his existence. Heugels issued *Chanson d'Ève* and *Pénélope ;* then Durand[1] followed with *le Jardin clos*, *Mirages*, as well as his latest chamber music (the first Quintet was published by Schirmers of New York). Decidedly, this was fame. He had never sought it ; it came to him simply by reason of the beauty of his music ; the reason that had led Dujardin-Beaumetz, on the excellent advice of Mme. Roujon, to nominate him as Director of the Conservatoire.

Fauré remained faithful to the *Société Nationale*. Nevertheless, this did not prevent him from encouraging the foundation of a rival society, the S.M.I. (*Société Musicale Indépendante*). It was in his study that was outlined a project, in opposition to the old pupils of Franck and against the supremacy then enjoyed by the Schola Cantorum in the *Société Nationale*, for the uniting of a group with wider sympathies. The name defines the aims : independence of cliques, dogmas and theories. More a wish than a reality ; total independence is very rare ! But it was linked with the aesthetic, at once liberal and traditional, of Gabriel Fauré. The new venture intended to accept, without bothering about tendencies, all works worthy of interest ; Fauré consented to be its president. As is well known, the first years of the S.M.I. were brilliant. Its very success incited the *Société Nationale* to a wider view, in the fruitful emulation which this rivalry produced.

During the war Fauré longed ardently for their fusion ; it was a real sorrow to him that this could not be brought about. But at this particular period there were such divergencies between the two committees that a union without autonomy could have led to nothing but a hybrid choice, turning away work of any significance from each side and admitting only academic music, devoid of character. Perhaps only the real presidency, active and dictatorial, of Gabriel Fauré or Claude Debussy, could have brought about the fusion in a profitable manner. But about 1915—supposing such a *rôle* to have been in his nature—Fauré had not the leisure for that ; his exacting administrative duties and his advancing age left him with neither the time nor the desire to take in hand a control, somewhat

---

[1] *We do not count* en Prière (1890) *nor the three earlier songs comprising* Poème d'un jour, *exceptionally published by Durand, and which are not numbered among his best works. As for Enoch, he had refused* la Bonne Chanson *as too dissonant and quite incomprehensible. This is no exaggeration ; the publisher himself confided this information to us, with no apparent regrets. It is true that at that time (about* 1895) *the work was still little known.*

" fascist " as it would of necessity have been ; and as for Debussy, he not only held himself aloof, but was already suffering from the cruel illness which was to carry him off in 1918.

To sum up, Fauré's musical sympathies were with the S.M.I. ; his disciples knew this well. And in his heart he never approved the change of spirit of the *Nationale*, which around 1910 had become almost a branch of the Schola Cantorum.[1] But old friendships (particularly with Vincent d'Indy), and the memory of all he owed to the *Nationale*—for he was never an ingrate—caused him to reserve for it the first performances of his second Quintet, the Trio and the String Quartet.

He had at last left the Conservatoire—in 1920. In the last two or three years his health had been impaired. His lungs had become more delicate ; no winter passed without an alarm. I was sadly struck in 1917 or 1918 to see him, who at the termly examinations had always seemed to us so robust and unchanged, grown thin, almost emaciated ; and though as lively in his mind as ever seized by a disquieting physical fatigue. A bad attack of influenza had aged him—had, who knows ? hastened his approaching end. And one dreaded to think that in a short time, perhaps, the swan would sing no more.

From 1920, as if in the knowledge that his life was nearly over, he laboured feverishly. His works, one after another, express that serene beauty his art had attained, and which was already noticeable in *Pénélope, la Chanson d'Ève*, and the second Violin Sonata. How unforgettable were the evenings at the *Nationale* which welcomed the second Quintet, the second 'Cello Sonata, the Trio . . . !

He was at that time spending his winters in the Midi, at Nice. But the erratic climate, with its sudden changes of temperature, was not always favourable. A serious attack of bronchitis brought him to the brink of the grave. " The lamp grows dim," said he one day. However, his natural vigour asserted itself, and he made a fair recovery. It is sad to reflect, but necessary to repeat, that Fauré's means were still precarious. The increase in the cost of living coincided with a sensible diminution of his income ; the State, in 1920, allowed him a pension which was quite insignificant. " Since Francois 1st is dead," artists of genius, in their old age, cannot hope to be welcomed as was Leonardo da Vinci by the " Roi dilettante."[2] The authorities could not be counted on ; it was necessary to make economies to balance the budget ! Well, it was better and finer thus ; for a great demonstration, the result of private initiative, united all his friends and partisans in the amphitheatre of the Sorbonne (June 20th, 1922).

Some friends of the master had had the idea of a concert for his benefit—with the co-operation of celebrated performers and the rendering of his finest works. The government willingly allowed the use of the hall ; and they recognised this as a national homage with the assent and presence of M. Alexandre Millerand, President

---

[1] *Which Fauré, it is known, scarcely liked. And probably his project for the fusion of the two rivals was not unconnected with a desire to balance the " scholastic " tendencies of the* Nationale *by the Debussyan or Faurian outlook of the S.M.I.*

[2] *Francois 1st, " le Roi dilettante," was also known as " père des lettres." (Tr.)*

of the Republic. Truth to tell, Fauré was not, is not and never will be a popular composer, like the writer of successful operettas ; one hardly dared hope adequately to fill the vast hall. But, backed by an intelligent publicity, the enterprise succeeded beyond all expectations. And not only the inquisitive, and the snobs, were there, but, with the still surviving friends of his youth (with many a touching reunion), there were the best of his colleagues, his pupils, and all musicians worthy of the name—and lastly, that whole host of obscure admirers won by the magic of his charm. And on this occasion M. Millerand was forced to reflect on the power of art, to reckon with the invincible force of beauty. Courteous applause had welcomed him. Soon afterwards Fauré appeared, and the acclamation was enthusiastic, unanimous, immense. Such moments are salutary in the history of art ; they give confidence in the future. It needs that—nothing less —so that a little optimism may support us in the face of Philistinism, too often triumphant. The audience, also, was perfect in comprehension and tact, applauding with an intelligent fervour, discriminating among the performers but reserving the major place for the master-creator and, in this diversified programme, distinguishing easily the best from the second-rate Fauré.

"What consoles me as I grow older," he wrote one day to his disciple and faithful friend, Émile Vuillermoz (thanking him for so many pages of a profound and subtle analysis) " is *your sympathy*." I imagine that on this memorable occasion the consolation must have come in the form of the certainty of survival. A comfort only relative, for he felt still so much creative force in him, knowing that the future would not allow him to realise his dreams ! But still, courageously, with indomitable energy, despite the wear and tear on his physique, the artist continued to live for his art. The summer came, and he went to the neighbourhood of Annecy, to the house of his devoted friends M. and Mme. Maillot. There were written the second Quintet, the Trio, the second 'Cello Sonata, and finally the String Quartet, which he never heard, the work not having been played until after his death. I had the good fortune, thanks to the kind hospitality offered me in this residence, to meet him again for a few days in July, 1923.

A large and peaceful country house in Annecy-le-Vieux, on the heights dominating the valley. The view from this hill is marvellous, over the mountains, almost Italian in the light and contours, fringing the blue waters of the lake dear to J-J. Rousseau. In the calm of evening the master would sit, contemplating the harmony and peace of the countryside. A truly perfect synthesis this—of Faurian music and the emotion of these closing hours, serene but indescribable ; the sun illuminating with soft light the tranquil summits silhouetted against the azure sky. There is indeed much happiness and much sadness in this divine quiet, in the almost celestial purity of the light, soft air ; under the shadow of night, how is it possible not to dwell on the painful end of the artist who perhaps to-morrow will be no more ? Doubtless, put into words, transposed thus into the realm of literature, these phrases seem to you artificially symmetrical, an ingenious correspondence between the countryside and the soul. However, I know well, as did every friend of Gabriel Fauré, that in these months when each day his work snatched something from death it was impossible not to feel a tender and cruel emotion, an almost physical pain which tore at the heart.

But in this contented house, in the beautiful garden, in the midst of kindly nature and surrounded by his affectionate hosts, Fauré appeared admirably confident and youthful in spirit. He remained in touch with the whole life of the nation—politically, artistically, literary. In the evenings he played chess, having learnt (when nearly eighty) this difficult game, with its imperious demands on the attention. He won with a naïve pleasure, and lost with a good grace. During the day he worked.

The last year, 1924, his weakness increased. He felt himself overwhelmed by extreme fatigue—but he overcame it, determined to finish his career with a String Quartet, a work which for a long time he had not dared to tackle, because (said he), " of the great difficulty of such a composition." Everyone knows this absolute modesty, a dominant characteristic of his gifted and rich nature. The night of its completion found him in pain ; forced to keep to his bed during the following days, he was taken soon after to his own house at Passy, in his apartments in the Rue des Vignes. Despite the most diligent care his condition worsened. Before leaving Annecy, however, he had found strength to write to one of the Vice-Presidents of the S.M.I. recommending the score of an old pupil, M. Le Boucher. His last days, in the intervals of respite which his illness allowed him, were devoted to the revision of the Quartet, the manuscript of which he confided to his faithful disciple and friend Roger Ducasse (2nd Nov.); with a final recommendation that it should be examined closely, to make quite sure that it was worthy of performance (sic).

" When I shall be here no longer " said he to his sons a few hours before his death, " you will hear it said of my work ; ' after all, what was it ?' on s'en détachera peut-étre. You must not worry about that. It is bound to happen . . . there is always a period of temporary oblivion. But that is of no importance ; I have done what I could . . . and now, judge me, O my God ! " Such were his last words. He died a few hours later, 4th Nov., at 2 a.m.

Everyone knows the " national " obsequies which were accorded him. But perhaps it is not so well known that this official recognition was not obtained without a good deal of parleying and negotiation. A very important personage indeed, when told of the death of the great master of French music, asked—his very words—" Fauré— who is he ? " A whole day was spent in discussions and evasions —then, finally convinced, the ministers gave way. The Madeleine Church, which for so long had resounded to his beautiful improvisations, was chosen ; his own Requiem pleaded for the clemency divine, and the orchestra also played the funeral plaint from Pelléas et Mélisande.[1] Words fail to express the emotions felt by the participants

[1]The ingoing voluntary was an improvisation by Dallier on the theme of the Élégie for 'Cello ; before the Requiem the tender and profound Nocturne from Shylock was played by the strings. The soloists in the Requiem were Mme. Jeanne Laval and M. Ch. Panzera, the excellent baritone to whom is dedicated l'Horizon chimérique.

# Gabriel Fauré

—his friends, at least ; though all were not there, for places had been
distributed by favour and not by merit. For many it was a question
of a rare spectacle, rather than a pious commemoration. This was
noticeable when, at the close of the ceremony, the noise of shuffling
chairs among the crowd drowned the grave flutes mourning Mélisande
and Fauré. Outside, the steps of the Madeleine formed a rostrum
from which several speeches were made. That of the Minister of
Education and Fine Arts, M. Francois Albert, left no one in ignorance,
this time, as to " who was Fauré." Among the crowd there was
less reverence ; one cannot expect the impossible. " All the traffic
must be held up, just for one man who ' kicks the bucket,' " grumbled
countless malcontents, in a Montmartre accent. No matter : everyone
could not know, or understand. The fundamental fact is the power
of this art, whose beauty finally imposed itself, definitely and beyond
all discussion, so that the representatives of the nation were forced
to such an act of homage to salute the memory of the most *musical*
of modern composers.

# Works

## Vocal Music *(Songs, Part Songs and Choruses)*

FOR A LONG time the master was classed as a " charming " musician, a song-writer, the " French Schumann." This is not true. Infinitely superior to the pretty ballad type, his songs are, however, not *Lieder ;* and as for the comparison with Schumann, it seems to us artificial.

In this genre there are some essential differences between him and the most celebrated Germans (Schubert, Schumann and Brahms).[1] With the composer of *Le Parfum impérissable*, there was no " popular " origin ; besides, from the time of *le Lamento* he quickly freed himself from the strophic form. In short, illustrative and introspective, he shows a French subtlety, very personal, and indefinable in a few words, which derived from his musical language, his taste, a certain reserve in the expression, and an imagination rich, diverse and precise ; one cannot compare his Song with the German *Lied*.

Not that he at once attained his ideal ; it is a far cry from *les Matelots* to *le Chanson d'Ève*, through *le Chant d'automne, Nell, Clair de lune, la Bonne Chanson, le Forêt de Septembre*. And this evolution presents some curious irregularities. If one studies the sequence of Opus numbers in the first collection one finds pieces clearly Faurian alternating with other compositions much less personal, the *Sérénade toscane* or *Lydia* anachronistically preceding *Rêve d'amour* (Op. 5), *Tristesse*, and *Sylvie* (Op. 6). Moreover, following the poems, the quality of his musical ideas changes ; and to an extreme degree, if he is one of those who really penetrate the text to the point of translating, almost unawares, even the weaknesses. Now Gabriel Fauré had this gift, amounting almost to genius, of identifying himself with the poets.[2] That is why, after the profoundly moving *Spleen*, and *la Rose*, infused with clearest paganism (1889), we are not astonished that *en Prière* (1890)—to some mediocre lines— is uneven.

Another characteristic of his evolution is the progressive abandonment of strophic repetition.[3] Not that this form was incapable of

---

[1] *And equally between them and Duparc, Claude Debussy, etc.*

[2] *At times he seems to go further, to penetrate deeper, than the poet ; he could then be said to reveal, by his music, a beauty latent in the text. Sometimes too—though more rarely—he seems to interpret it with a slightly more personal bias. In all other cases there is scrupulous fidelity to the intentions of his collaborator.*

[3] *The sense of the word*, progressive, *is easy to grasp. After some identical couplets* (le Papillon et la Fleur), *you will find some presenting slight alterations ; later, the plan of his songs becomes ternary (chiefly in the second set) ; finally, you admire a form quite homogeneous, wherein the idea, in development, is built up to a climax, as we shall see in due course.*

17

# Gabriel Fauré

beauty : witness the marvellous *Venise* of Gounod,—or *Lydia,* in its way a masterpiece. But it must be confessed that the generality of poems do not accommodate themselves readily to textual repetition— demanded of folksong, since the nature of primitive perceptions requires the repetition, *ad nauseam,* of the same things. And, from the musical point of view, it is certain that a well-ordered development, leading to the summit of expression, is more likely to be preferred, provided that the artist is cut out for the task. In the second set there are, strictly speaking, no couplets.[1] Even from the first set, *Chant d'automne* provides us with a veriable symphonic organisation iu miniature, as much by the plan as by the writing.[2] It is thus that Fauré, little by little, arrives at those perfect songs wherein the emotion becomes more intense in proportion as it makes more clearly for the final goal.[3]

1st Collection. We need not dwell on his youthful studies (Op. 1 and 2) : *le Papillon et la Fleur, Mai, les Matelots.* Their style is correct, the harmony pleasing ; the prosody (especially in the first of these) is open to question. Alone, certain modulations in *Mai* give us some inkling of the future, showing, with the influence of Gounod, a keenness of ear which is not negligible. The same qualities are to be found in *dans les Ruines d'une abbaye,*[4] slightly " *romance,*" but whose charm is perennial, with the naïve freshness of its musical idea, so youthful and ingenuous. The exact dates of these works are not known. " About 1865 " is given for this first set by the catalogue published by the *Revue musicale,* during Fauré's lifetime.[5] This is vague. One would rather suppose Op. 1 to be earlier than 1865, the year of *le Cantique de Racine,* whose technique and harmony is greatly preferable. On the other hand, the *Sérénade toscane* and *Seule* (Op. 3) we hold to be clearly later. *Seule,* nearer to Saint-Saëns, betrays the organist's craft ; as for the *Sérénade,* it is typically Faurian, with the characteristic tritone, reminiscent of[6] Marguerite's air from the Act in the Garden ! But could not one say, without malevolent irony, that Gounod's heroine sings here in the style of Fauré ?[7] The *Sérénade toscane* reveals already, in some charming details of writing, the feeling for Italy (an Italy of grace and fancy) which suggested to him some delicious music, right up to the time of *Arpège* (1897). We have good reasons for admiring Op. 4 : *Chanson du pêcheur,* and *Lydia.* Th. Gautier's celebrated *Lamento,* after the beautiful settings of Berlioz and Gounod, gave Fauré the

---

[1]*Even when the poem suggests it ; for example,* Notre amour, *where each strophe is different.*

[2]*We are thinking here of the movement of the bass, so solid and removed from the* " *song form,*" *which will be found towards the middle of this fine song.*

[3]*Cf.* le Parfum impérissable, Dans la Nymphée, *many a number in* la Bonne Chanson, *etc.*

[4]*e.g., on the return of the key of A Flat, by means of a charming and unexpected D Flat (bar* 8).

[5]Revue musicale, *October,* 1922.

[6]*Cf.* " O toi mon âme, ma pensée. ."—*For Marguerite's air the question is, how to end the act in the best manner. Re-read :* " Est-ce de plaisir et d'amour que la feuille tremble et palpite ? "

[7]*A similar remark applies to some passages in* Venise.

18

opportunity for ample development ; he eschewed the couplet form, in which he felt himself decidedly cramped.[1] In *Lydia*, Leconte de Lisle (or, if you prefer it, the good Horace)[2] again inspired him most happily. Even to-day, it is not without a poignant emotion that we read that adorable phrase, full of pagan resignation and voluptuous grace : " *Oublions l'éternelle tombe . . . laisse tes baisers . . . chanter sur ta lèvre en fleur . . .*" And the Coda, in its purity, so astonishingly simple, foreshadows the Greek artist of *l'Inscription sur le sable*, from *le Jardin clos*. Nevertheless, *Lydia* displays a *Latin* charm ; a nuance indefinable, subtle, but most decidedly perceptible. After this marvel one is astonished to find only a superficial pleasantness in *Rêve d'amour* (on Victor Hugo's well-known poem, "S'il est un charmant gazon . . ."). But here the composer was led astray by his fidelity to the text. It must be acknowledged that the incomparable interpreter of Verlaine was ill-served by collaboration with Victor Hugo. Too many factors separated them ; and anyway, the art of that prodigious word spinner was rarely suited to music. *L'Absent* (Op. 5, No. 3), is of a higher order of inspiration ; even so the somewhat theatrical dramatising of the poet accords ill with Fauré's nature. This was better suited by Baudelaire's *Chant d'automne* (Op. 5, No. 1), which makes up for *Rêve d'amour*. We have already remarked on the impressive development of this work ; it is illumined by that strange Baudelairian light which Duparc has realised, once and for all, in *l'Invitation au voyage*. Read it again, that it may not fall into an unjust oblivion. Op. 6 comprises three songs : *Aubade* (L. Pomey), limpid and ingenuous, anticipates *l'Aurore* of the second set ; but *Tristesse* drags, with its four stanzas ; and finally, on account of its banal text (P. de Choudens), *Sylvie* is not the best Fauré. Op. 7 seems to us much superior ; the rhapsodical nostalgia, the moving mastery of *Après un rêve* compels our entire admiration. Despite the disparity between their opus numbers it may well be that this lovely inspiration was contemporaneous with *Sérénade toscane*, both pieces being written on adaptations, by Romain Bussine, of some Italian poems. In *Hymne* there is, perhaps, a flagging of the inspiration ; the profound personality, especially, is less evident (despite some novel harmony, towards the middle). But the *Barcarolle* (M. Monnier) is one of those God-given inspirations, direct, immediate, which are the characteristic of genius.[3] No other music is conceivable to this poem, itself without much intrinsic value, but a source of beauty by the setting it evokes. The song must have been composed soon after 1870, the date of the *Tarentelle* (a Duet on some lines by the same author). In a few chords sustaining with their profound modulations a recitative of popular gait (but the popular style of the past ; before the art of the mob), there is all the infinite harmony of night time in Venice. What a magician, already ! The collection closes with Op. 8 : *Au bord de l'eau* (Sully-Prudhomme), whose progressions were

[1] *Cf.* " *Sur moi, le nuit immense plane comme un linceul. . . .*"
[2] *Much of Leconte de Lisle's poetry was modelled on Horace and the classics generally.* (*Tr.*)
[3] *Imagined, we have previously said, since Fauré became acquainted with "the Queen of the Adriatic" only much later.*

# Gabriel Fauré

daring for their time, and have never dated ; *la Rançon*, where, as with *Hymne*, it is a pity that Baudelaire has not inspired the musician as he did with *Chant d'automne ;* and *Ici-bas, tous les lilas meurent*, not without charm, but which does not impress as much as *Barcarolle*, *Lydia* or *Après un rêve*.

The dates of the lists which we have consulted indicate a long time between the first and the second volumes. But we have remarked that the former, to all appearances, extends over a period of several years ; from 1863 perhaps, to 1870 or even later. Besides, it is not reasonable to suppose such a long interruption in a genre which the master always held dear. " About 1880 " for Op. 18 ; 1882, for Op. 23—these correspond with the time of publication. But surely they were composed much earlier ? For consider : at the beginning of this modest organist's career there was no scramble among publishers for his manuscripts. After all, for those who know the slowness of "*père* Hamelle " in publishing his stock of music, it would seem quite logical that Op. 18, dating from 1876 and sold in 1878, may not have been printed until two years later—in 1880. But it is of little consequence ; let us come to the study of :

The Second Volume. *Nell* (Op. 18, No. 1), a marvel of grace, of an ardour voluptuously chaste, skilful in technique and supple in modulation.[1] *Le Voyageur* (No. 2) a dramatic Fauré, foreshadowed in a few pieces in the first volume. Ternary form, as also the succeeding *Automne* (No. 3). This shows a rare unity, a sound construction without a fault. The beauty of the vocal line, with its mounting emotion culminating in the final F Sharp, is supported by harmonies akin to those one finds sometimes in Saint-Saëns or Alexis de Castillon.[2] The three songs of *Poème d'un jour* (Op. 21) are much to the taste of singers ; charm alternates with a certain pathetic force, and the work concludes with a subdued resignation in which perhaps is seen the best of the work. Even so there is no comparison with either *le Secret* or *les Berceaux* (Op. 23). There is the same perfection in *les Berceaux* as in *Automne ;* no one knows better than Fauré how to reconcile diversity of detail with the discipline of a rhythm or design which is pursued with the most rigorous constancy. And the emotion is not any the less, indeed on the contrary. *Le Secret*, intimate, and so difficult of interpretation by reason of its restrained feeling, shows that the present scorn for Armand Silvestre betrays some injustice ; unless—a tenable proposition —it is held only that Fauré has transfigured these lines ? *Notre amour*, I confess, seems less happy, and the artificiality of the poem[3] has indeed proved an obstacle to the musician, despite the excellent writing he maintains. Op. 27 is again from Armand Silvestre : *Chanson d'amour* and *la Fée aux Chansons*, lively and charming (particularly the second) ; the grace of their unexpected modulations is Fauré's own. Not less attractive is *le Pays des Rêves* (Op. 39,

[1] *Cf. the return to the original key, before the final phrase,* " la chantante mer, le long du rivage. . . ."

[2] *Marie Alexis Vicomte de Castillon de Saint-Victor* (1838-73), *first secretary of the* Société Nationale, *and one of the pioneers of modern French song.* (Tr.)

[3] " *Notre amour est chose légère* . . . —*charmante* . . . .—*sacrée* . . .—*éternelle.*"

No. 3), with its indecisive rocking, tonal nevertheless ; and above all *Aurore* (No. 1), wherein reappears the youthful sentiments of *l'Aubade*, not without some subtle and profound melancholy whose contrasting shade makes even more brilliant, though with no harsh harmonies, the morning splendour of the return. " Trament de fils d'argent . . ." Decidedly, is not one compelled to admire the poet who could inspire such music ? But the gem of this Op. 39 is most assuredly No. 4, *les Roses d'Ispahan.* One wonders at the diversity of the composer ; his assimilation of the poets is such that one exclaims : these are not translations, but the poems themselves. A fantastical imagination would suggest to us, before so real an Orientalism, that this dreamy nonchalance sprang from I know not what Mussulman stock, contemporaneous with the Moorish invasion of the Midi. (Fauré's build resembled that of a peaceful Arab merchant.) But this would not explain how he showed himself worthy of Villiers de l'Isle-Adam by two admirable songs : *Nocturne* (Op. 43, No. 2), and *les Présents* (Op. 46, No. 1). They are held in insufficient esteem by the general public ; the profound mystery of the first, the elegance of the second, enigmatic and somewhat distant, though extremely sensitive, keep the masses at arm's length. Actually, they count amongst the most beautiful of the second volume.[1] The celebrated *Clair de lune*, also always moving in its apparent indifference, dates from the same period (Op. 46, No. 2, 1887). An Italy of imagination, music of flutes, mandores[2] and violas d'amore—a secret anguish which persists in the most harmonious perfection of harmony, line and rhythmic form.[3] But how pointless is criticism ! and how feeble one feels before the impossible task !

To the end of the volume there is no flagging.[4] *Larmes* (1889), with its wild augmented fifths, although slightly later than the Second Quartet (1886), shows some relationship with the image of the " smithy " which appears for the first time in the instrumental work. This striking song is hardly ever sung ; a hitherto unknown Fauré is revealed in these accents, extremely violent despite their rhythmic unity : a vigorous, bitter and almost romantic inspiration. *Au Cimetière* is not less violent in its middle section ; it enshrines the recollection of the peaceful country graveyard, seen in the clear air from the cliff's height. Points to note are the harmony, modal (plain-chant) and of a rustic humility, and the deep tenderness and immensity of it all,[5] in such a few bars. *Spleen* (" Il pleure dans mon

---

[1]*The order of this account has caused us to omit No. 2 of Op. 39, Fleur jetée, of a totally different character and, one would say, from its violent expression, earlier in point of time than le Pays des Rêves or les Roses d'Ispahan. But do not forget that a great artist is always multiple, and sometimes subjects mastered him rather than that he chose them. We see moreover in this work some vigorous modulations by which the musician enlarged his kingdom.*

[2]*Mandore, a small stringed instrument of the lute class.* (Tr.)

[3]*Cf. " Ils n'ont pas l'air de croire à leur bonheur. . . Et leur chanson se mêle au clair de lune."*

[4]*Except for* En prière, *albeit contemporaneous (1890). We have already indicated the reasons why this song is inferior to its neighbours.*

[5]*Cf. " Et peur avec de vrais regrets l'appeler par son nom."*

coeur "), one of the best interpretations of this celebrated poem, maintains a high standard in its intense melancholy, and how superior to Debussy's setting ! (Without setting up any other comparison, and while admiring unreservedly other masterpieces such as *le Colloque sentimental*.) Finally, *la Rose* (No. 4 of Op. 51, Nos. 1, 2 and 3 of which we have just noticed). In these few pages are a Mediterranean vividness, a harmonious and healthy paganism. And what extraordinary suppleness, what easy and youthful perfection, in solving so difficult a problem : fitting each word to the music without destroying the unity !

The second collection used to finish[1] with the two pieces of Op. 73, which the usual lists mention as being later : *Prison* (Verlaine) and *Soir* (A. Samain).[2] Is not this an error ? For we seem to remember quite clearly that they appeared before *le Parfum impérissable* (Op. 76). Rather one would place these compositions about the year 1895— before *le Parfum impérissable* (1897), and contemporaneous with *Pleurs d'or*, likewise inspired by Albert Samain. " C'est la pitié qui pose ainsi son doigt sur nous . . ." Certainly, he had already written pure, perfect, even very moving melodies ; and *la Bonne Chanson*, truly unique in intensity, had just been finished. But had he before, except perhaps in some bars of *En sourdine* and *C'est l'extase*, and the admirable D Flat Nocturne, ever sung with a voice so understanding and profound as in this phrase, which will for ever stir the hearts of Fauré's devotees ? *Soir*, the crowning achievement of the second collection, reaches the summit of tenderness and compassion. *Prison* is by no means inferior, though the two works have nothing in common. There is all the anguish of Verlaine, dramatic but restrained—and which everyone else save Debussy ran the risk of making theatrical : " Dis, qu'as tu fait . . . de ta jeunesse ? " The voice loses itself in the mists of memory, accompanied by a boldness of writing so truly necessary and direct that one does not notice the audacious perfection of the style.

Going back a little to the separate collections[3] : the songs " *de Venise* " (1890) and *la Bonne Chanson* (1891-92), both to texts by Verlaine, a favourite of the musician since *Spleen*. The first of these suites opens with a sort of homage to Watteau : *Mandoline* (from *Fêtes galantes*), of a witty and dreamy elegance, with momentary glimpses, almost nostalgic, over distant parklands, in the dim twilight of a moon " rose et grise." *En sourdine* and *C'est l'extase* reveal an emotion similar to that of *le Soir* of Samain with, in addition, something of the particular melancholy of the poet of *La Nuit de Walpurgis classique :* " Cette âme qui se lamente . . ." Undoubtedly, the inspiration of these two is on a high level, and compared with them *A Clymène*, though characteristic, pales somewhat

---

[1] *Nowadays, these songs (with* Larmes, Spleen, *etc.) form part of the third set—the second, like the first, containing only 20 songs.*

[2] Prison *and* Soir *figure in the old edition of the second set as Op.* 73, *and not* " Op. 83, (1900) " *as later lists indicate.*

[3] *Since this time the publisher Hamelle has issued a third volume of songs wherein can be found those* " from Venice " *as well as the* Madrigal *and the* Sérénade *from* Shylock. *The others will be noticed in due course, before* la Chanson d'Ève.

—and even the very charming *Green*. But neither Fauré nor Debussy discovered the extreme sadness buried by the " pauvre Lélian " under his fruits, flowers, leaves and branches. The whole of this album, with its frequent fragrance of the past, sad, calm and serene, merits its vogue among connoisseurs. But the rhapsodical quality of *la Bonne Chanson*, its extraordinary vital force, the passion of light and happiness and all the musical treasures it inspires, remains incomparable. Fauré preserved an especial tenderness for this work, unique in his existence for the optimism, the excitement, the kind of happy intoxication that persistently animates it. It is extremely varied, though a hidden and indefinable unity binds the pieces together. (1) *Une sainte en son auréole*, a stained-glass window where the musician's art follows step by step each word, nevertheless preserving a well-defined form. (2) *Puisque l'aube grandit*—like (6) *Avant que tu ne t'en ailles*, (7) *Donc, ce sera par un clair jour d'été*, and above all, (9) *L'hiver a cessé*—affirms Joy triumphant, with an expansive power the master has never surpassed.[1]  In contrast to this joy is the gentle tenderness of (3) *La lune blanche luit dans les bois* ;  the anguish, overcome in a superb final burst, of (4) *J'allais par des chemins perfides* ;  the breathless fever of (5) *J'ai presque peur . . .*, concluding with the passionate avowal " Je vous aime . . . je t'aime . . ." ;  the opening of (6), where the eager morning awakening of nature alternates with the uneasy fervour of the poet ;  and finally, the last lines of (7), " Et les étoiles . . . paisiblement sourirent aux epoux " :  a stroke of genius, for which he waited long weeks, until suddenly one evening he cried to his friends " I have it ! " *N'est-ce pas ?* (No. 8), no doubt, misses the youthful character, the candid confidence, of Verlaine's poem. This is not a criticism, but a simple way of stating a difference between the poet's conception and that of the musician ;  however, Fauré did suppress certain highly significant lines (" Quant au monde . . . que nous feront ses gestes ? . . . unis par le plus fort et le plus cher lien "). But the preceding has maintained an ample development. Finally, (9), *L'Hiver a cessé ;* here foregoing themes are picked up again, as in the finale of a Symphonic Cycle ;  a radiant ascent towards happiness (. . . met de l'idéal sur mon idéal ") makes a splendid finish to this passionately lyrical work.

It seems that after the successful effort of *la Bonne Chanson* Fauré experienced some apprehension with regard to new songs—as was only natural to an artist so anxious to do good work, so lacking in confidence of the value of what he had written. 1893 produced nothing, and the year following very little ;  only the harmonisation of *l'Hymne à Apollon*.[2]  No one was better qualified for this delicate

---

[1] *The same quality is found again* (evidently derived from la Bonne Chanson) *in the beautiful* finale *to the Second Violin Sonata. As for the* communal joy *of* Prométhée, *undoubtedly still more brilliant, its feeling is not more intense.*

[2] *Reconstructed by Theodore Reinach from an authentic manuscript, the longest fragment of Greek music then discovered. The first performance took place at the Hôtel des Sociétés Savantes, after a well-documented lecture by Reinach. Fauré, at the piano, accompanied one of his best interpreters, the late Jeanne Remacle. The evening concluded with some of the master's songs, when numerous empty places appeared. Doubtless an audience of archaeologists could appreciate only the music of two thousand years ago. . . .*

# Gabriel Fauré

task. His experience and his taste for the Gregorian modes led him to match this venerable monody with harmony most faithfully in the Greek style.

We have placed *Prison* and *Soir* about 1895. Op. 76 (*Arpège, le Parfum impérissable*) belongs to 1897. With *Arpège* we find ourselves again in the unreal gardens of *Mandoline* and *Clair de lune*. A wingéd rhythm of infinite grace, dreamy and tender nocturnal harmonies, the pure, unbroken and fanciful line of this reserved hymn to feminine beauty all combine to produce a work truly admirable—though with no pretence to the sublime. *Le Parfum impérissable* is more direct (" Mon coeur est embaumée d'une odeur immortelle . . ."). And in this case it can truly be said that Fauré *has* achieved the sublime. There is more of infinity here than in *la Bonne Chanson*, which sings of the present ; the work of Leconte de Lisle being of remembrance, a sort of haunting memory elevating the passion ; it concludes " beyond human time." Later, these appeals to a past of intense tenderness make themselves heard anew, in the Andante of the Second Quintet.[1] One can see that, in contrast to Victor Hugo (without falling into the error of comparing the two), Leconte de Lisle brought good luck to the interpreter of *Lydia*, *Nell*, *les Roses d'Ispahan*, and *la Rose ;* *le Parfum impérissable* is indisputably the finest of this collaboration.

There are no songs between 1897 and 1903, and even in other fields his output was less abundant.[2] The year 1900, it is true, saw the magnificent achievement of *Prométhée*. Op. 85 (1903) opens with *la Forêt de Septembre*, previously noted (page 10). He was now approaching his sixtieth year, and it is impossible not to hear the voice of experience in this noble meditation. *La fleur qui va sur l'eau* is full of undercurrents of inquietude, pulsing with tumultuous and dramatic vitality. *Accompagnement* soothes the mind—a nocturnal barcarolle, typically Faurian ; perhaps, however, without achieving perfect unity, for has not the musician, by a too scrupulous fidelity to the poem, missed some of the underlying meaning? In 1904 he returned, surprisingly, to his old collaborator, Armand Silvestre, with *le Plus doux chemin* (Op. 87) and *le Ramier* (without Opus number). But too many years had elapsed since *Aurore* and *la Fée aux Chansons*, and there is no doubt that he was no longer the man for Gabriel Fauré. *Le Don silencieux* (1906) gave him the chance to make a splendid return.[3] This work by the Director of the Conservatoire[4] was published by Heugel. Soon afterwards there is a new landmark in his musical life—*la Chanson d'Ève* (1907-10). Is it not paradoxical, that as the master grew older, his muse should grow younger ? He conjures up a golden age, the dawn of our Earth, the new-born, virgin life of a sunny paradise. And why not ? Would

---

[1] *Memories real, or imaginary—who knows ?—and it is of no consequence !*

[2] *These were the years of his Professorship at the Conservatoire.*

[3] *No doubt because it is contained in none of the collections, this song remains almost unknown. But rarely was the tenderness of the musician better inspired. Note too, from the same period, a charming* Chanson, *words by H. de Régnier.*

[4] *Fauré, as we know, was appointed to this post in 1905.*

24

the contrary have been more logical? Has not Arkel, in most
touching language, said much the same to Mélisande?[1] As death
approaches, man turns with increasing tenderness towards the memories
of childhood, or to the youth actually existing around him ; visions
of freshness, adolescence, charm, and—in the case of a fine artist—
purity crowd upon him. The inspiration, even the writing, of Fauré
was likewise purified—reduced to essentials, with an ever increasing
self-confidence. He was, moreover, extremely sensitive (cf. *Crépuscule*)
and weighed down at times with an anguish which brings out even
more strongly the primitive light, the pure atmosphere, of " the first
mornings of the world." The whole of this very beautiful collection,
the fruit of collaboration with the poet Van Lerberghe (whose too
early death is to be regretted), unified and diverse, like *la Bonne
Chanson*, merits discussion. But above all, the last of these, *O Mort,
poussière d'étoiles*—what a great and serene emotion is there enshrined !
It is impossible not to regard it as drawn from life ; the ageing man,
contemplating the beauty of night, musing on the fact that one day—
perhaps, who knows ? the next—his soul will dissolve into stellar space.
*La Chanson d'Ève* appears too infrequently at concerts ; the public
has no chance to apprehend its true worth. To be sure, its thought
is removed from the current fashion, if that fashion demands the
detestable syncopations of jazz, or only the diversion of the public
with picture-palaces and *trains-de-luxe*. But all this does nothing
to diminish the Faurian beauty of the work.

Le Jardin clos (Op. 106, 1915-18), likewise by Van Lerberghe, and
*les Mirages* (Op. 113, 1919) both prove to be of the same substance.
Fauré has confessed to us : " I can reckon on 20 years before any
one of my works is appreciated by the public."[2] It is true that the
fervent followers of his art, those who have troubled to follow the
course of its evolution, understanding this stripping away of super-
fluities and admitting that this apparently tenuous texture was capable
of very fine music, have not needed these 20 years. Nevertheless,
and despite the crowd of sympathetic listeners in the amphitheatre
of the Sorbonne, the number of initiates into this latest style is not
so great as one would wish. Perhaps the rhythm, shorn of accents
and seeking no violent contrasts, needs a little getting used to ; but
no true artist could resist bowing very low before those gleaming
summits : *Dans la Nymphée*, whose serenity interprets an intense
emotion, and which grows until it has filled all our being : *Je me
poserai sur ton coeur*, evoking by a subtle simplicity, with every note
in place, infinitudes of the sea and the soul : *Inscription sur le sable*,
of a pure Greek beauty which would seem to be " made out of nothing,"
were the intimate richness of this " nothing " not apparent : and the
extraordinary *Danseuse* from *Mirages*, which seems—with perhaps

---

[1] *Cf. Pelléas et Mélisande, " Et cependant les vieillards. . . ." (Duet, Arkel and
Mélisande, 4th Act.)*

[2] *This is an* average ; *la Bonne Chanson did not require so long, since towards 1900
it was widely discussed ; but the first volume of songs had scarcely won any notoriety
before 1885, and* la Chanson d'Ève *and* le Jardin clos *remain almost unknown even
to-day. It must be added that Fauré himself was careful to avoid any bitterness or
recrimination ; he merely stated the fact, with an air of tranquil resignation.*

# Gabriel Fauré

more apparent clearness, yet with quite as much mystery in the secret of its total perfection—a translation into music of certain pages of *l'Ame et la Danse*, by Paul Valéry. The remainder all partake of these same qualities, at once intangible and real, likewise also the last work,[1] *l'Horizon chimérique* (Op. 118, 1922) which becomes more attractive the more one knows it.

To the solo songs must be added a few part-songs.

Three Duets : *Tarentelle* (M. Monnier) and *Puisqu'ici-bas* (V. Hugo), dating from 1870, take us back to the Fauré of old times, but already one can admire the modulations, supple and sure. *La Tarentelle*[2] is a joyous Italian song full of rapid and agile *vocalises*, which one occasionally has the pleasure of hearing at pupils' concerts ; its technical difficulties save it from performance by the tyro, and only the most expert among the young ladies will risk it. *Puisqu'ici-bas* seems one of Fauré's best interpretations of Victor Hugo, without however offering the interest of the lively *Tarentelle*. *Les Pleurs d'or* is much later, from the period when the master, in the plenitude of his art, was discovering Verlaine and Samain. Here the music is most expressive, of a refinement and sensitivity almost worthy of *Soir*.

The original version of the *Madrigal à quatre voix* (A. Silvestre), often sung as a chorus, was designed for soloists. Written on the liturgical theme from Bach's Cantata *Aus tiefer Noth*, it should cause no scandal that Fauré has united this *motif* to some lines of a secular poet, and which with another interpretation becomes charged with a profound anguish. Note only the result, which is charming ; what grace, what suppleness in the vocal writing and the harmony ! This leads us to the *Pavane* (chorus with orchestral accompaniment), a more recent work, but of the same order. This is no pastiche of the 16th or 17th century, but the spirit of bygone times translated into a modern idiom which recalls the Modes of yesterday.

There are few other choruses in existence, except those we shall discuss in connection with *Caligula*. But we must mention *les Djinns*, a youthful work (1873, or perhaps earlier). It is astonishing that this work should be by him ; but one should remember to what extent the influence of Victor Hugo sometimes disfigures his style. It is hard to deny the grandiloquence at the crescendo, " Prophète, si ta main me sauve . . ." ; the harmony, moreover, is scarcely Faurian. It is in fact something of a freak. The excuse of its juvenility cannot be put forward, since *le Cantique de Racine*, as well as some of the songs of the first collection, most probably earlier works, preserve a character infinitely more in conformity with the master's personality. Quite otherwise is *le Ruisseau* (Op. 22, 1880), chorus for female voices, affecting and attractive, its modulatory lines studded with irregular resolutions. There is no need to return to *le Cantique de Racine*, since it has been commented on in the first part. At the time of the grand concourse at the Sorbonne it did not seem inferior, and one could give no better eulogy.

The religious choruses will be treated separately. There remains

---

[1] *The old man's collaborator here was a young poet killed in the Great War* (1914-18), *H. de la Ville de Mirmont.*
[2] *Dedicated to Mlles. Marianne and Claudie Viardot.*

finally *la Naissance de Vénus* (P. Collin), a kind of pagan oratorio (Op. 29, 1882). It is paradoxical, strange, but true that the master has sung the praises of the goddess better in some of his songs[1] than in this over-long work. One page of *la Rose* tells us more, and suggests more of the life and beauty of Aphrodite emerging from the briny wave, than all the musical commentaries accompanying the poem of P. Collin. Twenty years later it is probable that he would have written and even have thought quite differently. But there is no doubt that at this distant date Fauré had not the mastery which he showed so superbly in *Prométhée*. Perhaps also the text did not help him. However that may be, the vast and majestic monologue of Jupiter, and the vigorous chorus following it, seem more suitable for saluting another goddess (apart from a few passages more Faurian and genuine : "Reine du monde . . .", page 44). However, the work is not, at the opening, lacking in charm ; nor, as it progresses, in breadth. It would do great honour to a composer of the second rank. Being by Gabriel Fauré, one cannot forget that it falls short by some distance of those summits, *Prométhée* and *Pénélope*. This criticism, like that on *l'Allegro symphonique* and *les Djinns*, ought not to rouse the fervent devotees of the Faurian religion to indignation, but should be regarded as a sign of the sincerity of our admiration for so many other works, of an indisputable mastery.[2]

# Church Music

IT COULD WELL be maintained that the greater part of truly religious music of our age is to be found in certain chamber or symphonic works, or even in the theatre (for example, some of Arkel's music, in *Pelléas et Mélisande* ; while in *Pénélope* we recall the opening of the second act, where the feeling for nature is of the most exalted kind). This is surely superior to many of the superficial, saccharine, theatrical and sophisticated medleys for 'cello, harp and harmonium. But even so, there are still to be found a few great musicians devoting themselves to works for the Church, and such a one was Gabriel Fauré. His capacity as organist led him quite naturally in this direction.

The essence of his mystical quality was defined by Mlle. Nadia Boulanger in a remarkable article in *la Revue Musicale*[3] : "The Church may judge and condemn ; the master has never expounded this view,

---

[1] *E.g.*, la Bonne Chanson, *or* le Parfum impérissable.

[2] *We ought to mention, also, a charming* vocalise, *with piano accompaniment, written at the request of M. Hettick, which figures in the first volume of* vocalises *published by Leduc.*

[3] *The issue of* 1st October, 1922, *already mentioned.*

any more than he has striven to follow the dogmatism of the text. It might be said that he understood religion more after the fashion of the tender passages in the Gospel according to St. John, following St. Francis of Assisi rather than St. Bernard or Bossuet. His voice seems to interpose itself between heaven and men ; usually peaceful, quiet and fervent, sometimes grave and sad, but never menacing or dramatic."

Fauré's conception, all tenderness, pardon and hope, could not be otherwise ; it was in fact truly *Christian*, and opposed to that cruel anthropomorphism of a " divine justice " copied from the sententious reasoning of human tribunals. Particularly in the *Requiem*, the most well known and the finest of these manifestations, it is quite understandable that the indulgent and fundamentally good nature of the master had as far as possible to turn from the implacable dogma of eternal punishment. His doctrine, therefore, cannot be guaranteed inflexible ; but the only concern is the beauty of his music. We need not regret that his art could not tackle a detailed and minute picture of a hell which his heart could not desire when, thanks to the over-flowing of that heart, the *aeterna requies* is of such serene gentleness and consoling hope. The *Dies irae* appears, as it were, incidentally, and because it is obligatory (in a Mass for the Dead) ; moreover, it is quickly subdued by the return of the noble and almost confident prayer of *Libera* (No. 6). Other dark tones alternate with the light —*lux perpetua*—with which, by visions of angels and paradise, he prefers to illuminate this work, a greater than seemed at first to the fanatical Wagnerians. The *Introit-Kyrie* opens an austere portal— musical austerity which is not that of asceticism ; and everything macabre remains banished from this grief. The supreme anguish appears in the mysterious terror which hovers over the *Offertoire*, much more than in the ninths of the *Christe eleison* (page 10 of the score). By the simplest means, by the strangeness of unexpected modulations, and a canon wherein, enigmatic in their weavings, are intermingled the contrasting timbres of contraltos and tenors, the disquieting vision of an unfathomable lake cannot fail to be evoked, if not at length, at least in a manner extremely striking. But soon, what high hope—and how sure—is in the nobly tender pardon suggested by the *Hostias et preces* ! And the supplication of the chorus, on the initial *motif* of awe : *O Domine, Jesu Christe, Rex gloriae*, concludes peacefully in an *Amen*, pure and serene. Then, in reply, swells up the angelic *Sanctus*. The *Pie Jesu*, less heavenly but still religious in tone, expresses a piety most deeply felt and loving ; the *Agnus Dei* unfolds its pathetic prayer, its melodious and decorative curve (in the broad but sober style of the 17th century) leading, by a long crescendo, to a return of the first theme of the work, in D Minor. The same key, softened for an instant by the Major at the end of the *Agnus*, is also used for the *Libera*, to which succeeds the seraphic *In Paradisum*, worthy of Fra Angelico.

In addition to the *Requiem*, Fauré wrote a fairly large number of other pieces of a religious nature[1] : *O Salutaris ; Maria, mater*

---

[1] *The reader will find a complete list at the end of the work.*

*gratiae ; Tantum ergo ; Tu es Petrus ; Ave Maria ; Salve Regina,*
etc. ; also a Low Mass for women's voices and organ, of great purity,
consisting of *Kyrie, Sanctus, Benedictus,* and *Agnus Dei.* Two masters,
Bach and Gounod, seem to have been his guides. From Bach he
derived that beautiful contrapuntal writing, compact, pure, and free
in comparison with the narrowness of scholasticism ; from Gounod,
a delicate expansion whose sincerity never avoided the use of simple
chords, or naïvely expressive melodies. It is well known that Gounod,
at about the time that Charles Bordes inaugurated the meetings at
Saint-Gervais, was considering a Mass which would combine his
very real knowledge of counterpoint, his melodic gifts, and his naturally
tender inspiration, without theatricality. If he was not able to achieve
this work, one can say that Fauré, in some of his motets, in certain
pages of his Low Mass,[1] has become the successor to Gounod, giving
us what the composer of Faust had not the leisure to write before
his death. At the same time there remains the inimitable Fauré,
not only in resemblances to earlier themes,[2] but especially in almost
imperceptibly delicate shades of feeling.

On other occasions (cf. the *Agnus Dei* of the Mass, noble and
dignified) the style is almost austere. But as the music, on the other
hand, never surrenders its rights, this austerity preserves an inner charm,
exercises a secret attraction on our ear and our understanding. The
unfortunate habit of regarding Fauré as no more than a " seductive
charmer " is so widespread that perhaps the reader will be surprised
at the word " austere." However, there is no question that the gamut
of the Faurian inspiration extends so far. A whole volume could
be written on this aspect of his art, already noticeable in the first
collection of songs (cf. *Seule*), fully developed at the time of *Prométhée*,
and persisting, whenever the idea seems to require it, right up to the
time of the 'Cello Sonatas and the Second Quintet.[3] Curiously enough,
it appeared only rarely when he wrote for the Church. Then, in
general, charm was dominant ; a charm lovely, refined and easy in
its perfection, which reminds us of Renan. Impeccable form throughout, ideas full of a supple grace, " humanity " of expression—it is
hard to see that this is necessarily irreligious, and one would conclude,
with Mlle. Nadia Boulanger,[4] " To have given this to our unhappy
hearts, to have combined Charity with Beauty, Hope with Love, is
not this the most beautiful mode of participating in the work of the
Church ? "

---

[1] *For example, the* Benedictus.

[2] *To* Lydia, *for example, in the* Kyrie *of the Mass ; to* la Bonne Chanson, *in the*
Ave Maria (*Op.* 67, *No.* 2), *etc.*

[3] *Cf. first movements and finales.*

[4] Revue musicale, 1*st October*, 1922.

29

# Symphonic Music

IF WE EXCLUDE *Pénélope, Prométhée* and *Masques et Bergamasques*, intended for the theatre, also the incidental music to *Caligula, Shylock* and *Pelléas et Mélisande*, and on the other hand the *Requiem* and *la Naissance de Venus* which we have just discussed, Fauré wrote little for the orchestra ; moreover, of a total of three works, two have a part for solo piano. Mention has been made of a Concerto for Violin, a Suite for Orchestra and a Symphony in D Minor, which remain unpublished ; we believe even that the manuscripts have been destroyed by the composer. Nevertheless, the first movement of the Suite has been preserved as the *Allegro Symphonique* (Op. 68). Besides this we have the *Ballade* and the *Fantaisie*. Nothing more. No symphonic poem and, but for the *Allegro* and the *Fantaisie*, no example of absolute music.

One asks oneself why this is, when in his Quartets he has shown himself capable of sustaining, at length, ideas and conceptions which are in essence symphonic. There are several reasons. First, the difficulties which his times offered to symphonists. The great public and the authorities preferred the theatre ; the big concerts mistrusted the young men, even indeed those of riper years. César Franck was included in their repertory only after his death ; during his lifetime he had *not one* complete performance of his Beatitudes. One had to rely only on the sympathy of the *Société Nationale :* but this could give only one or two evenings of orchestral music a year—and these were necessarily first performances. Pasdeloup, Colonne, Lamoureux confined themselves to the classics, or Berlioz, or Wagner. As Florent Schmitt wrote : " . . . Prerogatives of the Dead, sole depository of genius."

Besides, Fauré's very nature, the reserve of his art, individual and intimate, demanding the epithet " intérieure,"—if this is, indeed, not incompatible with the orchestra, the style of instrumentalists accustomed to Wagnerian outpourings would find itself in opposition to a system of nuances at once modest and very sensitive (a sensitivity intense but restrained), which the interpretation of one of Fauré's works often demands. Sometimes, still unknown and without authority, the young musician would have to endure some passage disfigured by an " understanding " too superficial—affected, or unpleasantly expressive—something more serious even than a mechanical frigidity. It must be confessed that such conditions are far from encouraging. He would have persisted in this genre only if orchestral colour had been necessary to his inspiration. But in general Fauré's inspiration seemed best suited to abstract, almost unreal sounds, from which, paradoxical as it may seem, the idea of timbre remains excluded. And very often the orchestration of his music is uneasy. In the *Requiem* the deliberate adoption of an extreme sobriety does not induce monotony. But the same could not be said of the more colourful works. If you set about scoring *la Rose*, for example, the difficulty of preserving the sonorous unity with the varied colours of the different timbres will be at once apparent.[1]

If there must sometimes be brilliancy, nothing is more opposed to his art than picturesque, " amusing " sounds. Sometimes it is clear that the piano solo can render his thought. Fauré himself worked out the orchestral version of *Clair de lune*, which falls short compared with the admirable piano version. One can in fact say that the master whose vocal, piano and chamber music technique was perfect, was never completely at home with the orchestra[2] ; and then, the depth and refinement of his thought often demanded instruments unfortunately now obsolete, or nearly so—or if not, the handling of combined colours whose simple refinement conveyed his harmony. If the problem is not insoluble it remains very delicate.

For all that, the orchestral accompaniment to the *Ballade* (to all appearances written by Fauré), nicely balanced, supports the piano with discretion, even with poetry ; and it contains some charming combinations of sounds. Besides, the soloist remains the first consideration ; the score contains neither trumpets nor trombones. It would take too long to follow in detail the development of the themes, and such analyses, away from the music, bring nothing of great value to the reader. We will only remark that in this *Ballade* Fauré shows himself at once the disciple of Chopin and Saint-Saëns (". . . Cette fantaisie et cette raison . . ."). The background is an imaginary forest[3] whose myriad rustlings of fairies and sylphs accompany the soaring initial theme, limpid, grave and charming, like the love song of an adolescent Vigny.

The *Allegro Symphonique* is taken from the earlier Orchestral Suite, the other movements of which have not been preserved by the composer. A plain, almost scholastic, theme is accompanied by harmonies very different from those which, even before this early work, we associate with Gabriel Fauré. If it is less removed from *la Bonne Chanson* than, for example, *les Djinns*, it cannot be denied that this manifestation of the Faurian muse has had no successor. And it is difficult to regret it. Not because of its regularity and strictness[4] but because, after the fashion of some of the less good works of Saint-Saëns, it is more plastic than expressive. It would seem to have been a school task, never, I think, felt by the artist as an imperious necessity.

In contrast to this, the *Fantaisie* for Piano and Orchestra reveals on perusal a work of the most lively interest and power. It is played only rarely (we are even assured that, up to the present, it has had no more than *one* performance !).[5] M. Florent Schmitt has often

---

[1]*Though extreme brilliancy is not desirable, some diversity of timbre would be necessary in this song.*

[2]*Moreover, as has already been noted, he was not reluctant to entrust this work to some of his friends.*

[3]*We are assured that Fauré had in mind that of Siegfried; but without Mime, Siegfried, Wotan, or the dragon—and without Wagner. One should think rather of the atmosphere of " A Midsummer Night's Dream."*

[4]*Prométhée, and many passages in the Sonatas, bear witness to an inflexible disposition, but with infinitely more vigour and sensitivity.*

[5]*This, even if true in 1927, no longer applies ; the work has received an occasional performance by the B.B.C. (Tr.)*

deplored the unjust neglect of conductors and pianists in this regard ; we concur wholeheartedly in these reproaches.

The first movement is built on two themes : the first, virile, solid, boldly drawn ; the second, very simple, *à la Pénélope*, but full of charm and flexibility despite its bareness. The second movement, more agitated, relentless in its rhythm, remains obedient to the discipline which Fauré often imposed on himself during this last period of his life. The third part takes up again the opening themes, still more crowded with imitations, and brings the work to a close in vigorous fashion ; the form closely following Saint-Saëns, but enlivened by Fauré's individuality of expression. The development is never stifled by the deliberately canonical writing or the unity of the rhythm. The orchestration is temperate ; there is no seeking for effect, no " amusing colour," but one feels that it would sound well.

The times and, perhaps—on account of his modesty, already remarked on—his lack of confidence in himself prevented Fauré from writing a Symphony : but not the richness of his ideas, nor the breadth of his inspiration. The evidence for this is shown in this *Fantaisie*, so beautifully proportioned, a perfect example of pure music.

# Piano Music

THE PIANO WORKS have not the reputation of the volumes of songs—far from it. The concert world has scarcely accorded them the place that they deserve, a place unique in our music. The *Préludes* of Debussy, and Ravel's *Gaspard de la Nuit*, enjoy a more constant favour. However, setting aside their great beauty, the *Barcarolles* and *Nocturnes* of Fauré show writing as perfect as it is interesting ; there is no doubt that the master knew wonderfully well the precise resources of this much-decried instrument. But perhaps it is that they are less favourable to virtuosi than *l'Isle joyeuse*—or *Scarbo*, when the latter can triumph over this perilous Ravelian scherzo. It must be remembered, however, that one of the most illustrious, M. Alfred Cortot, persists in an admiration which he has expressed at length in an excellent article in *la Revue musicale*.[1]

The whole forms a considerable output : thirteen *Nocturnes*, as many *Barcarolles*, six *Impromptus*, four *Valses-Caprices*, three *Romances sans paroles*, nine *Préludes*, the *Ballade* (written in the first instance for Piano solo), the *Pièces brèves*, a *Mazurka, Thème et Variations*, and finally, *Dolly*, Suite for Piano Duet. " All those," wrote Fauré, " who, in the immense domain of the human mind, have seemed to use thoughts and language hitherto unknown, have only been expressing, through their personal sensitivity, what others have already

[1] *1st October*, 1922.

thought and said before them." This profession of faith is confirmed by the very titles of the collections—*Nocturnes, Barcarolles*, etc.—also by the nature of certain musical ideas, clearly traceable to such well known masters as Chopin and Mendelssohn (particularly in the first *Nocturnes*). But it happened as with the great painters of old, intent only on naïvely copying their master : despite themselves, if they had anything to say their art became personal and, without their knowing it, they achieved something new. So with Gabriel Fauré. Even in the traditional " accompaniment " figures he proves himself an innovator. Arpeggios, frequently replacing chords, intertwine with the melody ; their suppleness allows of surprises in the harmony, and does not hinder the ear from following the movement of appoggiaturas and passing notes which it may perceive therein. The hammering of repeated chords—as in a Chopin *Prélude*—does not seem to him outmoded ; and how right he was ! But a detailed analysis would detain us too long ; there scarcely remains room to comment rapidly on the works.

The three *Romances sans paroles* are early Fauré (1882), they take us back to the time of *le Ruisseau*. The young musician in the *naïveté* of his inspiration made no attempt to avoid Mendelssohn or Schumann. Moreover, he is recognisable already, by unmistakable signs ; especially in the third of these pieces, whose " romantic " character will doubtless appear somewhat *facile* to the proud who would like to admire only the sublime, something worthy of themselves. But, as with the good Chabrier, it is here so in place, and done so felicitously, that the evocation of this " autrefois sentimental " is one charm more. Happy the soul of the artist who knows not the fear of his first utterances being sincere and naïve !

The four *Valses-Caprices*[1] appear less subjective, one hesitates to say superficial ; but the musician has not given himself up to the contemplation of night ; the *salon* is as bright as day, conversation is gay, lively and animated. M. Cortot has well expressed it : " music so glib and sparkling, whose worldly nature is not glossed over." And he rightly praises their " sensual grace," their " perfect distinction " and their " impassioned tenderness." Moreover, these are not all youthful works, for the third dates from 1891, almost contemporaneous with *la Bonne Chanson*, and the fourth (1894) is catalogued Op. 62. Quite independent of their real value (the brilliant facility of Saint-Saëns here enriched by a grain of sensitivity, in just the right proportion for this style), they are esteemed as an exercise of lively and vivid inspiration. They restore the balance to a mind inclined, on the other side, to the Verlainian touch of melancholy.

The *Impromptus* play an analogous role in his career, and particularly the second, with its tarantelle-like rhythm, and the fifth, whose rapid semiquavers (in 2/4 time) anticipate those of the Scherzo of the second Quintet. The sixth is none other than a piano transcription of the Impromptu for harp, with, of course, virtuosity playing a large part —but without in any way becoming unmusical.

---

[1] *There is in existence too a* Mazurka *of an analogous character, but of less marked interest.*

# Gabriel Fauré

*Dolly* is at times allied to the *Valses-Caprices*, but a more introspective Fauré is often apparent. This charming album[1] was written as a sort of commentary on the games and pastimes of a little girl. Childhood is seen by each of us in his own peculiar manner. ( Debussy, in " Children's Corner," has described with humour the amusements of his dear little " Chouchou," as seen by a grown-up.[2] ) Fauré, while preserving his poetic feeling, seems nearer to the child : for instance, in the *Berceuse* with which the Suite opens. Who else, since the death of Gounod, could have written it ? This precise and dreamy simplicity, this writing at once artless and wise, seems the secret of the master. The combination of ingenuousness and refinement displayed by *Dolly's garden* (No. 3) and *Tendresses* (No. 5) will perhaps cause some surprise. A profound logic is concealed in the paradox ; if the woman can be discerned in the child, is it not at bottom most reasonable ?—correctly and subtly observed ? The mood of the *Valses-Caprices* returns in *Mi-a-ou* (No. 2), and especially in *Kitty-Valse* (No. 4), so full of animation. And the Suite ends with an astounding homage to Chabrier, *le Pas espagnol*, a masterpiece of gaiety, humour and solid architecture.[3]

One of Fauré's characteristics, and one which all the great masters have not possessed, was his extreme variety—the precious gift of passing from severe to tender, from grave to gay. Thus, such works as *Dolly* and the last *Valse-Caprice*, the *C Sharp Minor Nocturne*, and the *Thème et Variations* were in point of time very near neighbours. This last, in a form so difficult to treat without monotony, is second to none in beauty. It can be said that here Fauré has played the game according to the rules and won. The initial *motif* is presented with that vigour which too many of the ignorant deny to the musician of *Prométhée*. A noble melody, stamped with the clearness of an old coin. The Variations, while always pianistic and of the greatest interest from the instrumental point of view, are cast more than once in the form of counterpoint accompanying the original theme, a most useful means to the variety which is so necessary. It also forces boldness on the musician by the use of passing notes, and he proves himself here an incomparable master. Besides, the rhythms and harmony are so diversified that boredom is never present for an instant. The tenth Variation is a kind of scherzo, very quick, a veritable *tour de force* of modulation, and the work is rounded off by the eleventh Variation, most expressive, the harmony translucid and serene, tender, moving, consoling, peaceful ; (very beautiful Schumann, but from the second bar stamped with the indelible, original mark of Gabriel Fauré. )These pages, alone, suffice to place it without a peer in the literature of the piano.

The *Huit pièces brèves*, slightly later (in the maturity, almost the

---

[1]*Dedicated to Mlle. Dolly Bardac, the daughter of the lady to whom* la Bonne Chanson *is inscribed.*

[2]*And he adds, giving the impression of being a little detached from these games* " *with the delicate excuses of her father for what follows.*"

[3]*The Suite was orchestrated by Henri Rabaud ; this orchestral version was used to accompany an ingenious ballet (the story due to L. Laloy) at the Arts Theatre, under Rouché's direction.*

old age, of the master) nevertheless bear witness to a most significant youthfulness and freshness. But none knew better than he how to banish melancholy ; he was full of serenity, even vivacity, right up to the time of the second Quintet.[1] He had the rare and salutary gift of overcoming bitterness, of recovering his spirits after days of depression, as if some force of clarity and inner joy existed in the music itself. And no doubt this force did in fact exist. The collection of Eight Short Pieces, in the first edition (which we have before us) had no titles.[2] To go rapidly over these several pieces : No. 1, in E Flat, typically Faurian, reminiscent of the naïve tunes of *la Bonne Chanson*, but now much simplified, the writing very restrained ; No. 2, a pleasant *Feuillet d'album* ; Nos. 3 and 6, fugues in a simple and correct style, obviously less rich than those in the *Well-tempered Clavier*, and more careful, but whose reserve conceals an incontestable mastery ; No. 4, Andante moderato, serious, grave, at once firm and pliant, attaining real beauty ; No. 5, a sight-reading test written for the Conservatoire, less meditative than the foregoing, but how musical ! No. 7, a song, pure and gay, uplifted towards a sunlit sky, a youthful outpouring, full of happiness, foreshadowing the admirable finale of the second Violin Sonata, and the overpowering joy at the end of the first movement of the second Quintet ; No. 8, also included among the *Nocturnes*, less affecting than the sixth and seventh Nocturnes, but full of emotion and sensitivity.

The Nine *Préludes* (Op. 103) are almost unknown, both to the public and to most pianists ! I know of no injustice so great, unless it be the persistent disregard of the first Quintet, or the neglect by our concert directors of the fine *Fantaisie* for Piano and Orchestra—No. 1, in D Flat, an intimate Andante, a nocturne, of subtle and transparent harmonies—a golden evening sky above " les pins et les arbousiers " of *En sourdine* ; here are to be found also moving recollections of *C'est l'extase*, with the same refinement, the same clear atmosphere ; No. 2, as it were a paraphrase of the Opium Dream of Saint-Saëns' *Mélodies persanes* (a work certainly too neglected), a feverish whirling of dervishes, concluding, in a sort of ecstasy, with the evocation of some fairy palace ; No. 3, a barcarolle whose development, with its intentional tonal ambiguity, recalls one of the " Venetian melodies," *A Clymène*—though perhaps richer and fuller. No. 4 is a guileless *pastorale*, flexible, with succinct and refined modulations ; while No. 5 is emotional, violent, the very embodiment of rage. Then, as if reflecting on its own folly, its conclusion is painfully expressive, reminiscent of the *Libera* of the *Requiem* : altogether one of the most touching revelations of his inner self and, it would seem, an almost involuntary confession—troubled, yet at the same time carried out in the most perfect musical order. No. 6, a canon at the octave, supported by a solitary middle part. The writing here is strangely bold, in its implied passing-notes, with many a surprise arising from the inflexible discipline of

---

[1] *Cf. the charming and brilliant Scherzo of this work.*
[2] *Those which from time to time have been added will be found in the list of works at the end.*

the corresponding voices. No. 7, with the rhythm of *N'est-ce pas?* (from *la Bonne Chanson*) running through it, quietly passionate at first, then rising to fortissimo ; No. 8, in jerky and lively rhythm, is a vigorous scherzo ; and finally, No. 9, expressive, darkly mysterious, and recalling in places the *Offertoire* from the *Requiem*.

Apart from the *Préludes* of Chopin, it is hard to think of a collection of similar pieces that are so important. Richly and subtly concise, they bring us face to face with a human soul. Both form and writing are impeccable ; but these means are at one with the inner idea, and seem as if determined by it.

We shall return later to the question of Fauré's evolution. But for the time being let us assume that a division into three periods is logical.[1] " In the first," writes M. Cortot, " there is the fleeting, sensuous pleasure of his waking hours, the charming and glowing pictures of his dreams, the emotions and desires of adolescence." In the second period : " Later, up to the time of the ninth Nocturne, there is the emotional glow of maturity—the passionate and deliberate conflict of feeling." In the third period, comprising *Pénélope* and onwards, " an ineffable grave beauty, a restrained ardour, on which a purified and spiritualised musical style confers a sort of serene philosophy." " . . . the reserved and urgent eloquence of a harmonic language whose intensity seems to grow in proportion as it frees itself of superfluous ornamentation." This latest manner of the master, where the form grows from an inflexible but withal supple[2] logic, lends itself to the most diverse expression ; it would be dangerous to qualify this by the single word : *serenity* (that of *la Chanson d'Ève*, the Andante of the second Violin Sonata, etc.). It has already been suggested that this serenity is only the result of sometimes very violent eddies (cf. the *Prélude* in D Minor). And some penetrating words of M. R. Hahn supplement those of M. Cortot : a Fauré " ardent, uneasy, of fleeting tonalities and restless, modulating harmonies which quicken with a feverish circulation the inner currents of an irresistible and insinuating counterpoint."

The musician of the *Romances sans paroles*, *Aurore* and *Nell* (already more developed) is equally the composer of the first five *Nocturnes* and the first four *Barcarolles* ; which brings us to about the time of Op. 37. Still, the first Nocturne, in E Flat Minor, shows at times a striking and grave maturity, with typically Faurian harmony from the outset, over an accompaniment of chords, *à la* Chopin. A second, rather Mendelssohnian theme, over a growling bass, in sextolets, is followed by a very Venetian echo of the Mendelssohn Barcarolle. Note too the subtlety of the passing notes and appoggiaturas on the return of the principal theme. The openings of the second and

[1]*These periods, it is true, overlap to some extent, with no precise demarkation ; there are reminiscences and impressions of youthfulness in works later than* Prométhée, *and long beforehand there is the suggestion of that gravity which will move us so profoundly from the seventh Nocturne onwards. But on the whole the classification is just, and the characteristics clearly defined.*

[2]*The suppleness lies in the musical quality of the modulations and the harmonic progressions, in certain melodic lines, in delicate shades of meaning ; the order and logic are apparent especially in the vigorous themes, the canonic imitations and the finely proportioned developments.*

third Nocturnes affirm the simplicity of the impressions which crowd upon one in the calm of a beautiful evening. But the second has some very dramatic episodes, and the third some delicate harmony (where too, at the return of the melody, in the left hand, there are some resemblances to the middle portion of *Aurore*). The fourth also is founded on a very simple idea, of the *feuillet d'album* order, which makes what follows still more remote in its undulating " barcarollian " mystery ; then comes an expressive outpouring, exploiting the Faurian tritone. The fifth, whose opening phrase (like that of the fourth) remains " in the present," is developed by more refinement of harmony : the form, like the preceding, is ternary —the middle portion agitated and impetuous.

The first four *Barcarolles* date from the same time.[1] No. 1, in A Minor, in the same style as his setting of Marc Monnier's poem ; although never complex, already the harmony is thoughtful and flexible. No. 2, G Major, more lively, begins as a sort of serenade, but soon becomes more passionate, with the tonality strongly marked. No. 3, G Flat, inspired by Chopin to some extent, and from the first page much more liberal with modulations than the preceding ; and No. 4, A Flat, one of the best known, tuneful, quite short, perhaps more direct than the others.

An interval of some years—1886 to 1891—elapsed before Fauré returned to piano composition. This was the time of the *Requiem*, of *Shylock* and *Caligula*, also of the fine songs of the second volume. It was also the beginning of what we have called the second period of his art. From 1894 on were produced some new works for piano, few in number but of rare beauty.[2] First, the celebrated and excellent sixth *Nocturne*.[3] *La Bonne Chanson* has had a great influence on it ; one finds echoes of it in the passionate outpouring of the very first phrase. A new *motif* follows, with a syncopated accompaniment, concealing beneath its apparent tranquillity a persistent inquietude ; it is as it were a hesitant questioning, to which the reply (after the return of the initial phrase) is a lengthy development on a serene melody, subdued and contemplative ; this episode closes with a display of pianism, logically evolved, and leading to the recapitulation of the principal theme. But analysis is powerless to convey the real and profound vitality animating this work. As fine, and possibly even finer, is the grave seventh Nocturne, closely akin to the *Thème et Variations*, and also in the same key, C Sharp Minor. Here we have extremely concise but clear modulations and masterly part-writing. The opening already foreshadows that of the second Act of *Pénélope*, full of a great and noble melancholy. It seems that after the amorous effusions of *la Bonne Chanson*, Fauré's thoughts turned in the direction of the austere—always, however, realised in a most musicianly fashion ! For example, the *Thème et Variations*,

---

[1] *Nocturnes 1-5, from* 1883-84 ; *Barcarolles 1-4, from* 1883-86 ; *the second Quartet was finished in* 1886.

[2] *In the meantime there was the third* Valse-Caprice (1891) *and* Dolly (1893).

[3] *In the favourite key of D Flat; the key also of* Soir, C'est l'extase *and the first* Prélude.

and that lovely song, *la Forêt de Septembre ;* also, the fifth Barcarolle,[1] inspired by the stormy rages of the deep (" the sea, and the bold, free passion of an Antony and Cleopatra which these powerful rhythms awaken," writes M. Cortot).

The works of the third period, published by Heugel and Durand,[2] show an apparent simplification of technique.[3] There is an economy of writing, illustrated by the sixth and seventh Barcarolles ; the former is more moderate and tranquil in expression, the latter more restless and sombre, recalling *Crépuscule* (from *Chanson d'Ève*), and the syncopations which appear in a similar context in *Accompagnement* (" la rame tombe et se relève . . ."). The opening rhythm of No. 8, joyous and well-marked, soon gives place to an inner melancholy, also characteristic of the contemporaneous ninth *Nocturne*.[4] The Ninth recalls, as in a hazy remoteness, the happiness of the past. Much more tonal, with a certain sedate gravity (as if tired of the passion of *la Bonne Chanson*, whose influence nevertheless reappears in other works in this period), the Tenth Barcarolle preserves the monotony appropriate to a grey evening. No. 11, somewhat severe in rhythm, obedient to that constant discipline which characterises the composer's latest style, contrasts well with the Twelfth, allegretto giocoso (dedicated to L. Diémer), opening in an almost popular Italian manner from which, with the subtlety one would expect, he soon makes his escape. Finally, the Thirteenth and last Barcarolle, bare,[5] superficially almost dry, but at heart most expressive with that deep nostalgia for vanished bright horizons : sentiments that the composer suggests in passing rather than comments on in loquacious or theatrical oratory ; he seemed to desire to preserve the soothing and illusory serenity of the mirage.

Besides, this mirage is peculiar to the Barcarolle, Chopin's as much as Fauré's. That strange impression of unreal light, of the landscape reflected in a mirror, corresponds here to the very nature of the musical thought, which remains of a dreamy remoteness. By contrast, the *Nocturnes*, particularly the last ones, are more direct ; their expression is at least as profound, perhaps more so, but they are precise despite the suppleness of the harmony and, sometimes, of the melody.

The Ninth Nocturne, gravely charming, uses very few notes ; the luxuriance of the Sixth and Seventh seems romantic in comparison,

---

[1] *This* Barcarolle *dates from* 1895 ; Thème et Variations, 1897 ; *the seventh* Nocturne, *from* 1898.

[2] *With the exception of the sixth* Barcarolle, *published by Hamelle.*

[3] *In reality, the modulations have become extremely subtle—often very concise, or else unexpected in their harmony : and the use of retardations, of " échappées " (see note on page 68) and finally, certain progressions in the bass, musically logical but of great boldness, have combined to render this third manner sufficiently enigmatic to the non-initiates.*

[4] Accompagnement (*Op.* 85, *No.* 2) *dates from* 1903 ; *the seventh* Barcarolle (*Op.* 90) *appeared in* 1906 ; *the eighth* Barcarolle *and the ninth* Nocturne *were published in* 1908.

[5] *The notes reduced to a minimum, whence results the delicacy of certain translucent harmonies ; e.g., by a simple retardation in the bass, as in that beautiful song from* le Jardin clos *: " Je me poserai sur ton coeur. . . ."*

despite the classic sureness of development and the nobility of idea. It is built on a single theme, appearing first in a lower part, returning higher up the scale, and developed in periods repeated at the distance of a tone or semitone—a method dear to the composer from *Prométhée* and the first Quintet to the String Quartet, and which would perhaps be monotonous in musicians of second-rate phraseology, but in the case of Fauré the intensity of his expression makes it legitimate, and brings out the true value of the richness latent in this expression. Throughout these almost symmetrical periods the inner emotion grows and expands, working up effortlessly to a climax of great sonority, yet without disturbing the design or interrupting the persistent rhythm. The work ends in B Major with a most moving peroration, in a lyrical style inspired by *la Bonne Chanson*. Spiritually akin to the foregoing, the Tenth Nocturne opens with a very simple and slow-moving phrase, as it were made out of nothing ; but which grows magnificently, over a strongly moving bass line. Imitations between the bass and the treble, a few semiquavers—just sufficient for the animation of the *fortissimo*—and then comes relaxation, in the minor as at first. The following Nocturne, No. 11, " en souvenir de Noémi Lalo," a funeral elegy, calm and resigned at first, rises gradually to *fortissimo*, in accents of revolt against the young woman's death. There are some peculiar chord progressions, returning again and again to a characteristic cadence in one of the Greek modes,[1] ancient in spirit, but extremely modern in the audacity of its concise modulations. It remains a very moving work, quite as fine as the two preceding and perhaps more so, one whose mysterious tones reveal new beauties at each fresh hearing. No. 12 proves to be equally austere—grave and sombre, and at times enigmatic with its alternations of Major and Minor. Finally, the thirteenth and last, without doubt the most deeply felt and emotional, the finest of these pieces. It dates from 1922. At this period Fauré harboured no illusions concerning his age ; the present appeared to him merciless. There can be no doubt with regard to the first theme ; whether or no he intended it thus, it is his heaviness of spirit, his *age*, that is depicted for us, and with what richness of harmony—so simple, but how new and striking ! But now, a world of memories besets him, singing the extravagances of yesterday ; sudden glimpses of the past, infinite regrets—followed by a passionately impetuous episode, a renewal of life, even !—and then, relapse into the theme overwhelmed with age. Fresh bursts of energy follow, a pathetic exuberance ; some pianism, this time very prominent (despite the writing which, though never scholastic, is most correct) leads us to a *summum* of expression. Then —the conclusion, agonised, sombre—infinite lassitude and despair— the inescapable future which opens for him, the *aeterna requies*.

All this, we feel, is in this work, so direct, so profoundly human ; *expressionist* (so the modern aestheticians would describe it) even almost descriptive, and constructed with an incomparable musical logic and solidity of writing. Such pages, although little known

---

[1] *The Mode starting on E (Phrygian) : a notable example is to be found in Herod's Air " O misère des rois. . . ." from* l'Enfance du Christ (*Berlioz*).

and rarely heard, are not for the programmes of *virtuosi*—nor are they for the *salon*. One cannot imagine them offered to the ordinary public who, delighting only in empty virtuosity, dread any powerful emotion, above all sorrow. One would wish for no audience other than the friends of the composer, or the select few whose refined feelings and instinct for the beautiful would have prepared them for the understanding of this language of all humanity, vibrant, profound, but grave and mournful : much sadder in actual fact than the *Requiem*.

Besides, neither the Eleventh nor the Twelfth Nocturnes would survive the atmosphere of the brilliantly lighted concert hall, in the company of fashionable people who perhaps immediately afterwards would seek diversion in some night-club. Pianists should not ignore them for that reason ; on the contrary, they should get to know them and play them, either privately, or at concerts to carefully chosen audiences. They should make known these masterpieces—the *Préludes* also—to music lovers capable of appreciating them, and able in their turn to spread them round the circle of the initiates to Fauré's art ; for the majority of these initiates are ignorant of them. Such a desire is not, perhaps, quite incapable of realisation.

# Chamber Music

THE TRADITIONALIST SPIRIT ought not to be put off by one who, unpremeditating and even unaware, " a quarter of a century before other composers, spoke readily a prophetic language, with an ease, virtuosity and elegance which has not been surpassed."[1] One must take care, therefore, on noting that the Quartets and Sonatas of Fauré are conceived in broad outline on what is known as the *classical* plan.[2] Fauré has been careful, to quote again from M. Vuillermoz, not to " trace his plan from the sub-structure of a classical masterpiece," to " reproduce strictly neither the complete framework nor the details of the architecture . . ." " Fauré knew how to create new lines, unseen proportions and unsuspected balances, and his work is thus much more solidly constructed than that of those engineers eternally reproducing the same mass-produced ideal homes . . ." " He was the first to make us understand that one could—even that one ought to—create, each one, his own form."

Certainly, he was at bottom too good a musician to impose on his pupils the harmful tyranny of prescribed forms, or even to permit these slavish imitations. Nor in his works do we find any such

---

[1]*These and subsequent lines, in inverted commas, are taken from a remarkable article by M. E. Vuillermoz, in* la Revue Musicale, 1st *October*, 1922.

[2]*The customary meaning of this word, corresponding to the first movements of Haydn, Mozart and Beethoven, neglects the quite different construction of Bach and Handel's Sonatas, etc.*

servitude.[1] If he chose to respect customary usage, he, like Mozart, nevertheless preserved a freedom, an extreme flexibility, under an apparent obedience. It can be said that there was no modulation he would not use if it pleased him, if it sounded well, and if it seemed not untimely to his sense of proportion. But these excursions, far from a tonality to which he returned how and when he pleased, with the perfect grace of a cat falling on its feet, are analysable only by close study, by playing or hearing his music. We must therefore once again beg to be excused from following step by step the tonal evolutions of expositions and developments. It will be better to attempt to describe the works.

The first Violin and Piano Sonata dates from 1876. Without knowing the facts one would say that it was inspired by the much later work of César Franck. Indeed, the vehemence of the Allegro does show some affinity at times with Franck's second movement. But render unto Gabriel, and not unto " César," that which is Gabriel's. And, as sometimes with Mozart, on what distant horizons does the development open ! And to think that for some foreigners this art lacks depth ! The humour of the Scherzo is of extraordinary freshness, with tonal liberties very daring for the period. In the Trio, a graceful quietude reminds us (a rare thing for Fauré) of Schumann. The maturity exhibited in the Andante (fruit, perhaps, of Après un rêve) is at least the equal of the fine pages of " the classics." The feeling of anguish in the ninths dies down towards a complete serenity, overcoming this concentrated pathos ; the strongest and most moving serenity. The Finale brings us back to the light of day in a vigorous rhythm which the " second subject " is not allowed to enfeeble. Thus, a master stroke concludes this first attempt.

The two Piano Quartets have some traits in common, enough to justify their being studied together. Each opens, Allegro, with an energetic and virile statement of the opening motif, soon followed by the second, more flowing, theme, answered imitatively. Next comes the development, and then the return of the first phrase, this time harmonised in the gentle Faurian way. Is one justified in thus transforming a " masculine " theme—in metamorphosing it into a kind of misty memory, into nostalgic thoughts and loving regrets ? But why not, if it is done well ? The Scherzos, vigorous, fantastic, with their meditative Trios, contrast well with the great charm of the Andantes. In the first of these we have a broad and sweeping melody, succeeded by a song of infinite tenderness. The form is ternary, thus allowing for a repeat, slightly differing. The Andante of the Second Quartet opens with a mysterious sound of bells, in the bass ; the reply to this is a beautiful recitative on the viola for which, if it did not already exist, it would have been necessary to invent this noble instrument, so complete is the unity between its timbre and the very nature of its subject-matter. We cannot go

---

[1] It would, moreover, be vain to pretend that, because Fauré in the main adopts the classical scheme, Exposition, Development, Recapitulation, this thereby confirms the existence of only one possible Allegro movement. Other forms are allowable and logical.

into all the details of the spacious and pliant development of this movement ; but, at each fresh hearing, on the final return of the viola theme, we are transported far from reality, into a fairy-land—beyond the limits of the conscious. Sadness or happiness ? Is it indeed of this world ? One cannot tell. We need not seek to know, nor are mere words of avail—and I must be excused from having recourse to them. After these two very beautiful Andantes there is a risk of appearing less admiring with regard to the last movements. It must be admitted that Fauré is not at his best in Finales. Certain of the sonatas of Beethoven would seem to have been created for the development of a joy which carries everything before it ; we expect it, and are not disappointed. Sometimes again, we are ravished by an ingenuous cheerfulness, rustic and good-humoured. In Haydn and Mozart, too, there are some incomparable masterpieces ;[1] and if the conclusion of the C Minor languishes somewhat (in the recapitulation, and particularly in the return of the Second Subject), that of the Eroica remains without a peer. But rarely is Fauré so successful ; apart from the admirable paraphrase of *la Bonne Chanson*, naïvely lyrical, joyous and passionate, which rounds off the Second Violin Sonata.[2] Nevertheless it remains true that the Finales of both Piano Quartets do not lack for real beauty—nor even moments of pulsating life.

The First Quintet is almost completely unknown, and is very rarely played. Perhaps, at its first performance, it was not valued at its true worth ? Besides, difficulties of a material kind arose, connected with the exchange—for it is published by Schirmers of New York. But the need to rescue it from oblivion is urgent ; it is one of the master's finest works. It opens with a suave and strong theme, serene, noble, in an atmosphere of incomparable purity and luminosity. A grave second *motif* follows, given to strings alone ; and then we have some pathetic episodes whose eloquence (in their harmonic language and the design of the phrases) seem obviously of his *Bonne Chanson* period. It is quite likely that the Quintet[3] promised as Op. 60, but which never appeared (that is to say, between the *Mélodies de Venise*, Op. 58, and *la Bonne Chanson*, Op. 61), is none other than this Quintet : the first movement of which we have just spoken (to all appearances written during these fruitful years) is thus seen as a magnificent culmination of this period.[4] It might be that the Adagio is slightly later, contemporaneous with *la Forêt de Septembre*, certain harmonies from which here recur, from the second bar. This Adagio too is of great beauty ; extremely sparing of notes, and with great intensity of expression. Some characteristics of the later Fauré can be seen here ; viz., certain retardations, also the canonic Second Subject, so perfectly worked out that one forgets to admire the skill and mastery of style where each note seems to fall into place

---

[1]*Finale of the " Jupiter" Symphony, etc.*

[2]*Or better still, the Finale of the First Quintet.*

[3]*See the list of works at the end of the volume.*

[4]*We know moreover, on reliable information, that Fauré was long in finishing this Quintet which, numbered Op. 89, was published in 1906.*

quite naturally, without heed to the rules of imitative counterpoint, which nevertheless are obeyed perfectly. As for the Finale, cheerful, lively, and at first almost homely (without the least concession to the trivial), then firm and serious on the entry of the somewhat austere Second Subject, after which the youthful charm of the first idea seems even more sprightly, this movement is sustained with no weakness, strongly contrapuntal and rhythmic. Towards the end it is quickened and broadened in a transport of joy comparable to that in the last movement of the Second Violin Sonata—joy sincere, radiant, profoundly human—so rarely achieved by musicians—and so full of vital force.[1] But such expansive force in development, such admirable balance of youth and maturity, of mastery and lyricism, is to be found all through this Quintet—and especially in the conclusion of each movement. See, for example, the harmony on pages 29-30 of the first movement—and, towards the end of the Adagio, the intensity attained by a tenderness as deep as it is passionate—more concentrated even than in the Piano Quartets. This is explained by the fine writing—that perfection of style wherein form dominates expression, but without constraint (as is seen in the expressiveness of J. S. Bach).

In actual fact, we are here—together with the Second Quintet and the Second Violin Sonata—in the presence of one of the *first classics of our time*. This will be realised one day ; we can only hope that this day will not be long delayed.

The Second Violin Sonata (Op. 108, 1917) confirms Fauré's evolution towards an ever greater purity, towards that Hellenism betrayed by all his works since *Prométhée*. But—as always in the evolution of a great artist—the majority of his supporters refused to follow him. Even around 1895-1900 there were people to whom the first volume of songs seemed preferable to the second. There were the same complaints against *la Bonne Chanson* by the admirers of *les Berceaux* —and so on. It is not surprising that the Sonata of 1876 should be more favoured by violinists. However, if we had to make a choice it would fall on the second. Without knowing its date, one would judge it to be contemporaneous with *Pénélope*, if only because of the noble and tender Andante, whose convolutions answer each other like those of the fine canon which ends the first Act of the lyric drama. It will be objected that the *motif* was to be found in the Symphony in D, now destroyed. Granted ; but as a starting point. The real idea is the whole of the development, with the bold serenity of its harmonies ; this could have been conceived only at the time of *Pénélope*. The opening Allegro strikes a proud attitude ; people sometimes find it austere. Expecting of Fauré only mellifluous and gentle chords (a consequence of the reputation *le Secret* and *les Roses d'Ispahan* made for him), they are surprised, even disconcerted, by a force calm and sure, and moreover essentially harmonious. So much

---

[1] *It is strange that at the first performance this Finale did not command the admiration of the audience ; but if our memory is correct the work gave the impression of stopping abruptly. Was it perhaps that people expected four movements, instead of three ? Or was it perhaps that the opening of the movement was too quick and the development insufficiently powerful ?*

the worse for the uncomprehending ! As for the Finale, it remains, as we have said, incomparable. It is a magnificent climb to joyous summits, after commencing with a theme astonishingly youthful and ingenuous. There are obvious reminiscences of *la Bonne Chanson* ; but what a rich inspiration is needed, to make out of a single melody, *l'Hiver a cessé*, a whole Finale of a Sonata ! Fauré brings off this dangerous gamble with ease.

The two 'Cello Sonatas testify to an equal vigour, to the same virility of inspiration. Austere at times, always temperate, animated but superbly controlled, they will deceive listeners accustomed to the " swooning " of an instrument whose *chanterelle* too often delights in the accents of the operatic tenor. Fauré restores the instrument to its true *rôle*. The Allegro of the First Sonata is built on two themes : one, jerky, rhythmic, firm, suggests the air of warlike violence which Ulysses sings at the opening of the third Act of *Pénélope* ; a second *motif* succeeds it, simple, and expressive without insipidity. The same contrast is found in the first movement of the Second Sonata, the writing, in canon, even more compact, and ending in the major, glowing and happy. The two Andantes reveal great beauty : the first, on a pattern which may be found in *Pénélope*, leading to a calm and serene ending—a kind of Nocturne whose mood recalls somewhat that of the Second Violin Sonata. The Andante of the Second Sonata, in C Minor, opens after the style of the *Élégie* ; there is more of serenity, though—particularly at the point where arises the A Flat theme—so pure and consoling. The Finales, animated, vigorous and noble, end, in the major, with the same burst of light which one finds at the end of the first movement of the Second Quintet.

This Second Quintet is well known. Rare unanimity—almost everyone admires it, from MM. Louis Aubert and Roger-Ducasse to Georges Auric and Poulenc. Their approach, it is true, is through *Pénélope*. And certainly, at the first performance, it was with pleased surprise that people found such vigorous and youthful music in the veteran composer. Sympathy is necessary for the understanding of all his works, and above all for this one, whose Doric style (as we saw in the Second Violin Sonata) could be disconcerting from the Allegro onwards. This is built on a vigorous but extraordinarily simple theme, such as is to be found in *Pénélope*—on three notes— followed by nobly expressive cadences and retardations (as in *la Forêt de Septembre*). The development is spacious, its virile sensitivity never becoming insipid by reason of petty nuances.[1] Perhaps we see in this Allegro the finest first movement of Gabriel Fauré. The Scherzo reveals an incredible youthfulness, in its rapid scale passages and the light-hearted ease of its hymn to " la vie qui continue . . ." And from a man of his years, knowing full well that he must soon depart, this is more moving than one can say ! The Andante, even more, seems to revive the events that are gone. But, so intense, impassioned and tender in its long-drawn notes for the strings, it

---

[1] *Save, sometimes, under the hands of the performers. But this is not the fault of the composer, who took care to mark : ƒ sempre, for long periods. The performance should proceed on broad lines, with no fear of monotony which, by reason of the power of the inspiration, need cause no anxiety.*

reveals an extreme sorrow in this pleading with outstretched arms towards a past which will return no more. The depths of a heart still young—fiery torches burn there—the final glow, strangely revived, from fires about to be extinguished. And we remain gripped in a meditative sadness before the apparent calmness which reclothes, in its musical perfection, a poem till then unique in his artistic career. As for the Finale, likewise firm and brisk, what was said of the Piano Quartets applies here. It ends less brilliantly than the Second Violin Sonata or the First Quintet.

The Second 'Cello Sonata, analysed with the first, followed just after. Then came the Trio for Piano, Violin and Violoncello. It seems to us spiritually at one with the Second Quintet, especially in the Andante ; it is perhaps as beautiful, though more reserved and constrained in tone. Its charm is incomparable ; the balance of timbres and tessituras, so difficult to achieve in this medium, is without a fault. As for the writing, it is of amazing subtlety ; as in *l'Horizon chimérique*, each note has its part to play, and says more than would be thought possible.

The String Quartet is the equal of the masterpieces in this genre. It forms a worthy conclusion to this series, though there is no doubt that the Finale is not equal in value to the other movements. But in these, what profound melancholy—the expression of a final farewell ! Not that the inspiration falters for an instant ; but one would say that here is the traveller on life's journey, bowed down, at the end of his resources, infinitely weary, abandoning himself to fate. " Go thy way, youth of humanity ; I go no further, awaiting death to-morrow." He saw departing towards the future, disappearing over the horizon, all his companions and fellow travellers. Had Fauré any idea that all this would be apparent in his work ? We do not know. Sometimes the subconscious discloses thoughts one would never confess to. No matter ; here, in the most beautiful language, is the symbol of that final lassitude, and the presentiment—without bitterness, but with the most painful resignation—of an end not to be long delayed. In fact, it came immediately the work was finished. But one should not be deceived in the underlying meaning. " All here is *joy* and serenity," wrote one critic. No : this perfectly realised serenity cannot deceive one, and it is impossible to forget the sadness that it masks.

# Miscellaneous Instrumental Pieces

TO THE SONATAS and Quartets are added a number of shorter works :

For Violin, the charming *Berceuse*, well known, but a work one hears again and again with undiminished pleasure—a sign that its simplicity is not empty or trivial. The *Andante* is catalogued Op. 75 ; one would imagine it to be earlier than compositions with neighbouring Opus numbers. The nature of the harmony, the very character of the expression makes us think so—notably the middle portion, then the rather Franckian development and the repeat, *ff*, of the first theme.

For 'Cello, there are some pieces of charm (*Romance in A*) or of virtuosity (*Papillons*) : not unpleasing, but certainly less worthy of preservation than *l'Élégie* (Op. 24), a renowned miniature, with its beautiful, grief-stricken phrase whose nobility is the equal of that in the Andante of the First Quartet—also in the same key of C Minor.[1] The middle section, in the relative major, is very expressive, as affecting as the second theme of the Allegretto of Beethoven's Seventh Symphony. The first theme is then repeated, *ff*, and is followed by a Coda on the second *motif*. The whole piece is finely wrought and beautifully balanced ; orchestrated, its beauty remains unimpaired.

The *Sérénade* (Op. 98) likewise for 'Cello, is too little known. Charming, witty, soaring, with touches of *Mandoline*, more Venetian than Spanish, it would figure worthily in the score of *Shylock*.

Mention must also be made of : the *Romance* (Op. 28) for Violin and Orchestra ; the *Sicilienne* for 'Cello and Orchestra (Op. 78) ; the *Fantaisie* for Flute and Piano (Op. 79) ; and a little unpublished piece for 'Cello (Op. 49). The *Impromptu* for Harp is the original version of the sixth Impromptu for piano.

Finally, there are various transcriptions (for Violin or 'Cello) of songs or piano works. But they are not due to Fauré ; moreover, there is nothing to show that, in his inner heart, he approved of all these arrangements, on which we will dwell no longer—except to mention the skilful adaptations for Piano Solo by M. Alfred Cortot, of the *Berceuse*, from *Dolly*, and *la Fileuse*, from *Pelléas et Mélisande*.

---

[1] *It is remarkable how with Fauré the same tonality is often used for the expression of similar sentiments. Compare the* Libera, *from the* Requiem, *with the ending of the* Prélude *in D Minor.*

RAMEAU DID NOT approach the theatre until he was fifty ; Fauré delayed still longer before *Pénélope*. We cannot regret that he waited until he had attained mastery ; how many there are who, too soon, have plunged into an art they considered lucrative, indulging in carelessness and mediocre ideas which do nothing to conceal the inexcusable bombast—in a word, an art of inferior quality under the pretext that a " theatrical style " is necessary, and that a phrase requires a special grossness before it will get across the footlights. The error of this unhealthy tradition is demonstrated by *Figaro, Boris Godounov, Pelléas*. . . . Music is a whole, and there is no need for the theatrical style to be opposed to that of the symphony. Fauré's trump card was to have understood this. It does not follow that the wife of Ulysses will express herself like the poet of *la Bonne Chanson ;* and already the voice of the *Pie Jesu*, pleading eternal rest, has been distinguished from this ; no one was more master of these nuances. But they are never contrary to the regard for *good writing ;* they never destroy the unity of a style which, always, proclaims itself the best.

Unity is necessary. This salutary axiom determined the subordination of the drama to the expression of feelings. In the lyric theatre, the movement comes from the spirit, and not from sensationalism or operatic splendour. That truth, misunderstood by all those who used to find that the Garden Act from Faust dragged, and clearly proclaimed by the third Act of *Tristan*, or the fine Duet of Arkel and Melisande, Fauré did not fail to observe in composing *Pénélope*. By these excellent principles (also dictated by his musical good sense), this masterpiece stands apart from the mediocrities on the " prix de Rome Cantata " pattern, which weighed heavily all their lives on many laureates of the Institute. But luckily for him, Fauré was never at the Villa Medici.[1]

Finally, one important gift was his—a gift denied to many famous musicians. Less truly " theatre-minded " than Fauré (despite the current opinion), their language never varies, their invention does not correspond to the diverse characters of the *dramatis personae*. In contrast to this, Fauré's melodies revealing a profound poetry with a supple precision, so perfectly apt, it was not to be doubted that he would succeed—even though he had not the " experience " of an old hand, though he disdained the tricks of the stage and paid no respect to the conventions : or rather, *because* he remained outside this artificial and sophisticated art, which was not the *true* music drama.

He began with incidental music ; then, in *Prométhée*, which approached nearer to the lyric drama, he used large choral forces,

---

[1]*Without indulging in the pleasure of paradox, it can be stated as a fact that the finest lyric dramas of the Modern French School are due to artists who have held aloof from this competition, or who—like Debussy and Paul Dukas—have renounced as completely as possible the style and customs of the theatre.*

and even tragic actors (the Gods). In these accents alone there was already the augury of the success of *Pénélope*.

The score of *Caligula*[1] permitted only a small number of pieces for orchestra alone : interludes and ballet music. The most important part consisted of the Four Choruses for Female Voices, so rich in that Faurian power of suggestion, whose nuances depend on imponderables.[2] Here there is no doubt of the period or the place—the Rome of the Decadence. Certainly, the charm is antique and pure, the harmonies deliciously sensual : " Winter flies away." But—since it would be out of place here—the curves of the phrase have not the sort of proud, Hellenic attractiveness of the canon, at the end of the first Act of *Pénélope*. An infallible and subtle taste guided Fauré in paths which, though similar, were sufficiently divergent for the distinction to be perceptible to cultivated minds. The contrast between " *Heures guerrières* " and " *Heures heureuses* " is of the same bas-empire, as well as the vocal antiphony of " De roses vermeilles . . .", and particularly that fine invocation to voluptuousness with which the work ends : " César a fermé sa paupière . . ." Intoxicating odours ; heavy, fleshly and majestic drunkenness of a surfeit of pleasure—civilisation debauched by luxury. From the first Scene of *Salomé* Richard Strauss, in his realistic manner, gives us the uncomfortable mustiness of a corrupt society—already nauseating. In this there is certainly a kind of genius ; but—the music to *Caligula* remains beautiful, and on a par with the beauty of antiquity.

*Shylock* is a free translation which we owe to the distinguished talent of E. Haraucourt, and it is a matter for regret that it has had to wait so long for a revival. It is impossible to put into words the Venetian charm by which this score suggests, for the *Madrigal*, the scenes of Carpaccio, homely or worldly—and for the *Sérénade*, the picture of elegant gondolas and delightful palaces of pink marble. " Forbidden kisses, it is God who ordains them," sings this *Sérénade* : a profession of faith which seems to be Fauré's, as it was Debussy's —to write what the " adorable Goddess " suggests—and what if there are crimes such as to call forth an official report from Harmony's village policeman ![3] As for the *Nocturne* for strings alone, it is impossible to place this music, so profound and universally human is it. The intense tenderness of night here revealed[4] was one of the most beautiful incentives of Fauré's inspiration, contrary to the general opinion, which sees him by preference only the painter of clear, noonday waters (an artist so diverse cannot be classified in this narrow and precise fashion).

---

[1] *Written, it will be remembered, for the revival of Dumas' play.*

[2] *Note the difference between the tone of some of the religious pieces, and that of analagous secular works.*

[3] *This " statement " does not imply that Fauré, previously, had not been bound by scholastic discipline ; and the fifths which he allowed himself were never acts of petulant rebellion. The purity of style remains intact ; we shall refer to it again in the chapter devoted to his technique. But from the first it is necessary to avoid any misunderstanding.*

[4] *Cf. the similar pieces for piano, and the* Nocturne *on Villiers de l'Isle-Adam' poem ; also that fading twilight which opens the second Act of* Pénélope.

*Pelléas et Mélisande*, given in London in 1898, was accompanied by incidental music conducted by the master. The *Prologue* is less a " decor " than a state of mind ; that forest wherein Golaud discovers Melisande appears to our understanding as a legendary atmosphere —a symbol of the sensitivity soon to be crystallised in the grief of the young girl, mourning the enigmatic crown which the huntsman descries across the water " which is not very deep." The second theme voices this distress, and lasts until the curtain goes up to the cries of Golaud. *La Fileuse*, with its two contrasting *motifs*, is like a paraphrase of *le Rouet d'Omphale*, of Saint-Saëns, but more concise and refined. (However, you will not like it unless you can forget for a moment the Melisande of Claude Debussy.) In this episode Fauré's conception of the heroine is of someone much nearer to ourselves ; we do not say " coquette," but there is a kind of juvenile and almost malicious gaiety—on which account no doubt his colleague never appreciated this really charming interlude.[1] But with Fauré, despite his expressive depth—and the subtle melancholy of his interpretations of Verlaine—there remains a *naïveté*, an ingenuousness,[2] which seems to have forsaken Debussy at about the time of his *Nocturnes*. We will not dwell on the *Sicilienne*, which, though delightful, was written for a later occasion, and is scarcely related to the rest. The last piece (preceding the fifth Act) reveals a poignant emotion—quite different from that of the lyric drama, but not less beautiful. The " Golaud " theme reappears, powerful, tragic ; the dull, intense anguish of this Finale, so simply achieved, attains an extraordinary inner pathos.

In order to finish off the shorter works let us anticipate a little, and deal with *Masques et Bergamasques*, posterior to *Pénélope*. The scenario, by M. René Fauchois, was inspired by Verlaine's *Clair de lune*—from whence the title was derived. To a number of Fauré's early works (*Clair de lune*, naturally ; the *Madrigal*, the *Pavane*, etc.) incorporated into the action, were added some interludes written later, and whose style is not without similarity to Mozart—a new departure for the composer. Of course, he had for long appreciated at his true value the musician of *Figaro ;* but his inspiration (if not his technique and his artistic principles) had usually remained fairly remote. In *Masques et Bergamasques* on the contrary, the resemblance extends to the nature of the ideas themselves, sometimes even to the harmonisation. A charming tribute to *Cosi fan tutte*, which however was not easy to bring off ; nothing less was needed than the touch and mastery of Gabriel Fauré.

Finally, before studying his two works for the theatre proper, we must mention the incidental music which he wrote for Georges Clemenceau's *le Voile du bonheur*. Doubtless it was not perfectly suited to his character—which, with the musician of *Shylock* and

---

[1] *It may be recalled here that, in the London orchestra, the number of strings was cut down. In performance at symphony concerts the excerpt loses something of its lightness by reason of the considerable number of the strings.*

[2] *Cf. The Finale of the Second Violin Sonata. Accents of great innocence are also to be found in some of the works of Debussy's adolescence.*

*Caligula,* was always the case. The score, however, for what reason we know not, remains unpublished ; and since we have not been able to hear it, we must be excused from devoting to it anything but these too brief lines.

The circumstances which governed *Prométhée* have already been told. Being of a very special nature, they have deprived the public of a real knowledge of this superb work. Those composers, few in number, the fortunate elect who heard it at Béziers, must have been able to realise that the Paris performances gave only a feeble idea of its power and incomparable splendour. In the vast Hippodrome a performance (with full orchestra) only threw into confusion sonorities too loud for a confined space : it needed, most definitely, the open air, which favours the full blast of great masses of brass, never confused, never needlessly strident. Later, at the Opéra (re-scored for the occasion : but then, without the brilliance we would have desired) the *mise-en-scène* of the first Act seemed illogical : while the Chorus was singing of a joy more than human, and just as we were expecting to see them flood-lit with brilliant lighting, a veil of material[1] was interposed between the audience and pulsating Humanity acclaiming the discovery of Fire. These veils were removed only towards the end of the Act ; they quite spoiled the effect, and were contrary both to the composer's ideas and to the real life of the work. And all the rest suffered from the absence of the burning sunshine over the Arena. To crown all, in the theatre the declamation of the text seemed interminable. At Béziers, the fact that it was in the open air kept people patient and in a good temper ; one made up one's mind, for good or ill, to accept the traditional monotoning delivery.[2]

In *Prométhée,* the poets Jean Lorrain and M. A.-F. Hérold made an attempt to revive Greek tragedy. Speaking and singing were used alternately ; the latter was reserved for the Chorus, also for all the *rôles* of the Gods. The conception was not lacking in grandeur, nor, after all, in logic. Speech was limited to the human characters. They spoke, no doubt, at rather too great length, and this error of balance —not an unusual fault—makes the musical portions of the work all the more appreciated.

The drama opens with a *Prélude* of unusual power, constructed on the " Prometheus " and " Fire " *motifs.* They are piles of Cyclopean blocks ; but the soul of the Titans is transformed by the art of Apollo. A sovereign Reason guides it. And already, is not this the pure aesthetic of the Greeks ?

The Prelude leads without a break into the opening Chorus of the first Act. The scene is rugged, wild, mountainous. Men and women rush excitedly from all parts : " Eia, eia, hasten from the depths of your caves ! " They are celebrating the arrival of the " mystery bird," the bird of Fire. " It is about to take the air," cries one of the Chorus, " and it is thou, Prométhée, whose glorious cry will rise

---

[1] *Light curtains, but through which the performers were seen as it were through a mist. Even their voices were muffled.*

[2] *But it is a hindrance in these lines which, despite a certain " literaryness " are not devoid of beauty—a fault which Aeschylus, with his absolutely simple lyricism, never committed.*

to greet it ! " This Chorus, vigorously rhythmical, with its repetitions so essential to the nature of the work (an open air style, broadly painted) —this evocation of a primitive, prehistoric humanity, by the same pen which sang the Verlaine melancholy, was so manifestly contrary to Fauré's customary usage that even some of his disciples (though not those present at Béziers), did not understand it : " Too solemn," said one of them to me.[1] But there is not a single page that does not reveal Gabriel Fauré, whom by certain harmonies it is impossible to mistake. He is here absolutely himself ; more powerful, indeed, than ever before—moreover, with no pomposity, but with a fine breadth of touch, easy and free. Note particularly a number of Passing Notes (on page 18, E Natural against E Sharp ; page 19, G Flat against G Natural) bordering on Bitonality, discreetly suggesting a civilisation not yet fully developed. In the Béziers Arena, triumphant, a challenge to Fire was made resplendent by the ringing voice of the tenor Rousselière. He unleashed the enthusiasms of youth with an irresistible force, and in the whole Faurian output we know of no more superb lyricism, wherein the refinement of unexpected —but appropriate—modulations never excluded the use of older techniques, such as the six-four (page 25, second line). And this is the real boldness—from which springs the true power, so convincing on a single reading that one is astonished that the whole musical world even yet has not recognised it, with affectionate but humble respect.

The first Scene continues, in a more agitated rhythm, on the initial Titan's Theme . . . " Prométhée is Power ! " And the Perfect Cadence (page 29) proves in its turn that there are no such things as obsolescent harmonies or progressions, but only two sorts of music : that which grows old, and that whose spirit remains imperishable. And what pure charm, always vigorous and noble, in the soaring soprano solo : " Prométhée is also Hope ! " Finally, the invocation to the happy future concludes (over an energetic reference in the bass to the Prometheus theme) on an unexpected chord, opening on to untold horizons of mystery, in a species of religious terror (page 40, 7th on G Natural, after the sparkling tonality of A Major).

The Titan enters. This scene is spoken, not sung. Enthusiastic and boisterous, he shouts of the joy of his discovery. Just before the

---

[1]*If we have insisted more than once during the course of this work on the force of Gabriel Fauré, it is precisely because of that reputation of " musicien charmant " to which many of his critics, even among his friends, are in danger of confining him. Camille Benoit compared him " a tous les points de vue " with Grieg! (Cf. the quotations from M. H. Imbert and M. O. Séré.) M. J. Poueigh, under the pseudonym of Octave Séré (" Musicien français d'aujourd'hui '') wrote the following lines on the subject of Prométhée : " One feels decidedly that Fauré's muse is as it were frightened (sic) by so much shouting and by all this instrumental violence." And it was none other than M. Emile Vuillermoz, however lucid on other occasions, who could mistake the profound Faurianism of this powerful tragedy : " He has put more of his soul into Soir than in the whole of Prométhée." (La Revue Illustrée, 1st July, 1905). Such also was the opinion of his most fervent admirers in the face of Pénélope and the Second Violin Sonata. It is remarkable, on the contrary, how Fauré has always remained himself, his Muse growing naturally to the dimensions of his subjects. But in order to discern this, a previous initiation is necessary ; one must know the works well, and not judge them too lightly.*

end of this monologue Pandora enters. " Plucking up courage, she approaches Prometheus, and arrests him with a supplicating gesture."[1] The music is resumed : a theme of three notes (A, D, G in descending 5ths) accompanies Pandora's entrance. But her fear does not stop the Harbinger's ardour. He climbs towards the rocks. Then arises " a woman of austere countenance, draped in long veils. With outstretched arm she tries to stop Prometheus." Gaïa, the Titan's mother, reminds us of the ancient Erda of the Ring. Her spacious, solemn and moving admonition seems like the transposition into Faurian terms of the prophecies of the original Goddess who appeared to Wotan. But you will find no reminiscence, nor the least inferiority in the later work. This superb air, its harmonies inspired by maternal anguish and imperious commands, need fear no comparison with the best of Wagner. It seemed to me at once more concentrated, more solid in development, fuller and *richer*.

Prometheus repulses Gaïa. He repulses Pandora. Encouraged by the Chorus (here the beautiful expansion of the Prelude returns, in counterpoint on the reappearance of the theme), the Titan goes on his way. He climbs the hill. Reaching the summit, there is a flash of lightning : " a branch brandished by Prometheus catches fire."— " Men, see the gift I promised you. See the Fire ! "—" Horror ! " the people cry : Prometheus, thunderstruck by Zeus, is hurled down. " Behind the rock have risen a God and Goddess of wild aspect, Kratos and Bia. Between them is Hephaïstos, the divine smith." With a scornful and biting cruelty, they give in detail the particulars of the rebel's punishment. Here comes again an extraordinarily bare theme, followed by a menacing ascent in the bass. The scene, very freely carried out—following the evolutions of the script— nevertheless preserves a perfect unity. Kratos and Bia order Hephaïstos to lead away the silent Titan, and this first Act comes to an end with the evocation of " whirlwinds of snow and sleeping winters " wherein " Zeus desired the tortures of the indomitable Prometheus to be confined."

At the beginning of the second Act there is a digression, but one whose musical beauty is such that the interest does not flag for an instant. Pandora is dead. A long procession of women and girls accompanies her funeral, some carrying the body on a bier of leaves and branches . . . Those who have not heard, in the Arena at Béziers, the calm, heroic voice of the trumpets, far away, diffusing their three notes into the serene air—and the noble anguish of the harmony alternating with the tolling of the funeral bell, pure and clear—can have no conception of the evocative power of this scene. And from the top of the rocks there winds a procession, a living bas-relief, antique, pure—while at the same time Chorus and Orchestra uplift a great plaint of grief, of virginity—of death, light and youth all at once—through which there flitted visions of the companions of Artemis, chaste huntresses, flying headlong through the mountain forests. Ode to the dead maiden, wherein Fauré at times closely approaches Euripedes, and which crowns an Olympian pleading :

---

[1] *The words in inverted commas are taken from the librettists' own directions.*

" Tu passais, royale et sacrée . . ." (page 91) ; words are powerless to describe its divinely pagan beauty. Then the Chorus replies, telling of the deathly darkness of Hades, " a country where lurks a dumb people . . ." " Pandora is a tiny ghost—and the ghost outstretches her thin arms. Only the memory of Aède keeps her still in the light."[1]

" The women have hidden Pandora in a cave in the mountain. They steal away across the rocks. Prometheus appears, on the top of a very high boulder, between Kratos and Bia. Hephaïstos is with them, carrying chains, nails and a hammer." The ensuing scene is the one where, against his will but obedient to the chief of the Gods, Hephaïstos finds himself compelled to chain the Titan, his brother, to the rock of the Caucasus, where Zeus' eagle is to come pecking his liver perpetually regenerated. The invective of Bia and Krastos—truly withering—contrasts with an air of the pitying brotherly God, full of deep and noble compassion : " O sublime et bon Titanide " (page 101). What restraint there is in this development—the theatrical accent, so inappropriate, completely banished ![2] Then the Smith sets to work and, to music of extreme bitterness, prepares the punishment . . . " He is now chained." " And thou," replies Kratos, " thou canst continue thy insolent cries. Weep, Prometheus—weep and wail."

Left alone, Prometheus gives vent to his sorrow (this is the admirably lyrical Aeschylean invocation : " Éther divin . . .") There is some uncertainty in the next scenes, words being provided only for one air sung by the cruel Bia. The intentions of the librettists are not sufficiently clear ; having caused Pandora to die (the pretext for the fine funeral chorus, and which we cannot regret), she is restored to life to satisfy the needs of the drama. And perhaps, dramatically, a certain tediousness results, since Bia's air, striking though it be, adds nothing to the force of the preceding scene. But Pandora has reappeared at the threshold of the cave, swathed in her funeral robes, she glances round her, hesitant. Brusquely, Bia stands up and stops her with a gesture : " Go ! Zeus forbids thee to approach." The Act ends with the lamentations (spoken) of Pandora.

The action is resumed from this point in the third Act. The young maiden calls upon the Oceanides : " Tell the Titan there is one who still loves him—that, in the night whose shroud your hands sweep away, he is not alone." This, three times repeated, alternates with spoken dialogue, wherein Pandora cries aloud her hope—and Prometheus his fears. The choruses are of gentle, feminine tone, whose charm occasionally recalls the Fauré of la Bonne Chanson and other songs. However, after Pandora's restoration to life, if the composer is not to blame, nevertheless the work suffers a little by being too fragmentary and episodic. The first Act formed a

---

[1] *The writer adds here a note to the effect that " the meaning of these somewhat enigmatic words is rather obscure."*

[2] *This was not to the liking of the Bass singer responsible for this rôle : he wanted to finish on a high F, instead of the middle A Flat, so submissive, so incapable of all resistance, drawn out with an infinite sadness. If one has a fine voice, what a pity not to reveal it !*

complete whole ; quite half of the second, also (Pandora's funeral, the binding of Prometheus) showed a spacious and simple dramatic conception. After which, by contrast, the interest is divided between Pandora, Prometheus and the Oceanides ; musically, too, the effect is somewhat dispersed by the number of separate pieces, of slighter dimensions—and which moreover are interrupted by spoken dialogue (thus, Interlude—Bia's air—conclusion of the second Act—Prelude to the third—the three Oceanides Choruses—and, finally, the dialogue, sung, between Kratos and Bia). There is no doubt that all this engendered a feeling of indecision, an impression of over-long expectancy.[1] Given the structure of this drama on broad lines, with the opposition of spoken word and song, these pages suffer by being cut to a slighter pattern. As for the music, despite the pellucid charm of the harmony, the threefold song of the Oceanides cannot be compared with Pandora's funeral music ; and the adjoining scenes, with Kratos and Bia, being not *more* prominent than the excellent ones at the end of the first Act and in the middle of the second, actually seem *less* so, by reason of the gradation which our mind demands. Very little is needed in the theatre to produce the impression of dragging (especially when the musical portion has just been interrupted by the spoken word).[2] And perhaps Fauré, realising, with his unerring taste, this fault in the larger design (even if he would not admit it), had less enthusiasm for the composition of interludes which performance would render less significant.

This is, however, merely an hypothesis ; and if some inequality is in question it is only in comparison with the summits. It is clear that it is relative ; none of this part is without charm or vigour. However, from Scene VI in the third Act, the musician comes into his own again, making a brilliant return. " At the very top of the mountains Zeus and the Olympians appear. With them is Hermes, holding a casket. Everyone rushes to the spot at the sound." Over a tremendous roll on the kettle-drums, the " Gods " theme blazes out on the brass. Here is absolute simplicity—a canon at the 5th, over the percussion, long sustained. Wherein lies its superhuman grandeur ? In the character of the theme itself, embodying such a vital, dominating force ; in the part played by the bass note,[3] on which the chord is built ; in the peroration which, modulating from E Flat to C Minor[4] broadens still more ; in the change of interval on the repeat of the canon (now become a canon at the 6th) ; in

---

[1] *It was more damaging in Paris than at Béziers, by reason (as explained above) of the " optimism," the tranquillity, free from impatience, which performance in the open air induces in the public.*

[2] *We do not say, too little action. It would sometimes be the opposite. Here it is felt to be irresolute, disunited, superficial—more theatrical than Aeschylus. It aspires to movement with Pandora's supplications, and by the double veto of the Gods. These episodes perhaps harm each other ; a complete, Aeschylean simplicity would be more suited to the flow of the music. It is, moreover, only the slightest dip between the peaks. The remainder of this fine poem is fashioned on broad lines, and serves the musician admirably.*

[3] *It produces a chord of the 6th on the G of the drums ; much more spacious, in its vagueness, than the immediate and clear-cut root position chord.*

[4] *Giving a six-four over the G of the drums.*

the modulations, which animate the following Recit. (of Andros, pp. 161-164) . . . If this dry analysis gives no idea of the music, neither does the score, at this point, suffice. But imagine the vast sweep of the Arena (in the fading afternoon, the sounds of nature dying away, the orchestra more and more impressive)—filled with the immense sonority of trombones overriding the thunder of the drums—the blaring brass mounting to heaven where one can visualise the Olympians themselves, resplendent . . .

Prometheus counteracts the ruse (the casket Pandora is to receive contains, as you will remember, all the evils which will spread over the earth). But no one believes the Titan ; his prophecy is in vain. Pandora, with the fatal gift, descends towards the crowd. " The grave Gods have smiled on us—the way is clear where thou goest." This is given to the chorus, in an ineffable phrase of youthful hope, a phrase whose every harmonic inflexion deserves analysis, wherein all is pure, grave and charming as in " The Temple of the Wingless Victory." From here the work drives on to its conclusion in a crescendo incorporating elements of the Prelude, amplified, and which is developed in a majestic omnipotence to be compared only with that of the last scene of *Götterdammerung*. And note that Fauré is not belittled by the comparison. No : this music of the Acropolis fears the proximity of no mediaeval City, however gigantic. Here, Zeus is as grand as Wotan. The inner robustness of these harmonies has the compactness of marble which defies the ages. And the Olympian order, the supreme *logic* of this essentially *sensitive* lyric art, are clear and definite facts.

So, as splendid as it is well-proportioned, this work is one of the finest in modern music—we might say, in *all* music. The only causes for regret are the *longueurs* at the end of the second act and in the middle of the third, and the special open-air conditions most decidedly necessary for *Prométhée* to shine with its complete brilliance ; thus performances in an ordinary theatre are hindered from realising its whole beauty. I know not if it will ever be performed under the Hellenic sky ; it awaits it and cries out for it.[1] But on the day of its revival at Béziers its splendour will be reborn, incomparable.

A considerable time separated the *première* of *Prométhée* from that of *Pénélope* (1900-1913). But having lived with Aeschylus, the Titans and the Gods, Fauré could not forget Greece. It constantly inspired him : in the very form, in the conception of his art. Thus *la Chanson d'Ève*, *le Jardin clos*, and the Second Violin Sonata bear the mark of the Attic influence. Finally, there was *Pénélope*. More than the Iliad— perhaps too persistently warlike (even though he might have written, I think, an admirable setting of the last chant, and though the prayers of old Priam might have found in him the most sympathetic interpreter)—

---

[1] *And why should it not be presented in the Greek theatre (modelled on that of Epidaurus) of Berkeley University, near San Francisco ? America's resources in the matter of first-class orchestras and the possibility of producing great choral works there make this wish less Utopian than it appears ; the chief obstacle is that the reputation of* Prométhée *(and of Fauré generally) in foreign countries is not to be compared with its value as a work of the first order.*

the Odyssey tempted him. Besides, he had no desire to accentuate the archaism ; what purpose would it serve ? Prehistoric times had inspired sufficient of his pages for him to have no need to treat an adventure of Homeric times in the style of Rochegrosse's violent picture " la Prise de Troie." (After all, *Pénélope* remains substantially epic, and even brutal where necessary ; witness the end of the second Act.) But rather, let us say that, in the musical speech of our times, a civilised artist, of the time of Pericles[1] tells us of the return of Ulysses. Is the postulate admissible ? Yes ; the work being there to justify it, and whose beauty, *inwardly Greek*, assumes the form of modern harmony and melody, without the least disparity, in the most complete unity of conception and style. He is not interested in erudite science concerning the ancient Modes, nor cold architectural reconstruction ; in short, there is no false primitive or artificial roughnesses, seeking (as puerile as vain) a vigour which would, on the other hand, banish charm. Fauré remains, constantly and sincerely, *himself* ; but at bottom his inspiration is Greek in that he has drawn the most faithful and human pictures of Penelope, Ulysses and the Suitors. And his power is bound closely with that sincerity which makes the work so vivid and profound. As already a sympathetic bond had been established between his art and that of Athens—from 1900, with *Prométhée*, and onwards—the arrival at this new summit of musical civilisation, *Pénélope*, was natural and quite unforced.

The poem, by M. René Fauchois, does not pretend to be so *literary* as that of *Prométhée*. Ought one to complain of this ? And if so, why ? It is clear, with no out-of-the-way words, broadly designed— and since it is the framework of this refined, strong and perfect music, there is no need to regret the choice—when a libretto less sparing in incident, rich in poetic licence and precious in vocabulary might, who knows ? have done the composer a disservice. In the next chapter an attempt will be made better to define this harmony between Greece and Gabriel Fauré ; it must suffice here to describe the drama.

The exposition is entrusted to the first three Scenes. But first, the Prelude has introduced, positively, heroically, the figures of Ulysses and Penelope. Heroic indeed is the noble waiting, the sublime fidelity of the wife in her invincible hope ; and likewise is the music. At the height of Penelope's exaltation appears the " Ulysses " *motif*, distantly at first—of the same Doric simplicity which has already been displayed in certain outlines, almost linear, of *Prométhée*. The whole of the development is founded on these two themes.

Scenes I, II and III. " An ante-room to Penelope's chamber. As the curtain goes up her maids are discovered, spinning. Some, weary, have let fall their spindles. They yawn and stretch themselves, and move to lift their drapery in the background. Then one becomes aware of the blazing sun."[2]—The Chorus explains the situation : Ulysses, gone these twenty years ; the Suitors gradually invading

---

[1] *And not of the time of the Anthology, of which Claude Debussy's perfect setting of les Chansons de Bilitis reminds us.*

[2] *The words in inverted commas are taken, with minor alterations and omissions, from the stage directions.* (Tr.)

his house; Penelope tirelessly faithful. And the serving-maids protest that, in their mistress's place anyone else would have given way.—Enter the Suitors, brushing aside the drapery. They insist on seeing the Queen, who is cloistered in the adjoining room. A lively altercation follows, for the aged Euryclée opposes their demand.

Scene IV. Penelope appears, at the top of the steps. Everyone moves back. She proclaims her hope : the Gods will protect Ulysses ; if Zeus decides so, he will return—this evening, even. The Suitors give a cynical contradiction ; for them, the exile will never return. However, they are uneasy ; the shroud intended for old Laertes, the warrior's father, which the Queen promised to weave before choosing a new husband—what a long time it has been on the loom ; why is it not finished ? Discreetly, she avoids the question. But, says Eurymachus : "From now on you will work under our supervision." At this point (at a sign from Eurymachus) flute players and dancers come on the stage, while the intruders crowd round Penelope. In despair, she launches a last appeal : " Ulysses, faithful husband . . . come . . . relieve my distress ! " And then from without comes a voice in reply. It is Ulysses, disguised as a beggar, old and unrecognisable. He seeks hospitality for the night. He is welcomed, despite the hostile Suitors. Arm in arm with those servants amenable to their desires, they go off. Man and wife remain together : a certain vague presentiment remains unclarified ; she does not recognise him, and confides him to the care of the old nurse. Taking advantage of her solitude, Penelope has unfolded Laertes' shroud ; she proceeds to undo the work she has done during the day, as she has done every night before. But the Princes are spying on her ; she is discovered, and this time they decree : " To-morrow, she must choose one or the other. There must be no more delay." The last night has come . . . Once more, still hopeful, Penelope decides to climb the hill commanding a view of the sea, eager for the appearance of the vessel so long expected ! Her guest, returning with Eurycleia, requests to accompany them. " . . . Take my cloak, old man ; the night is cool." " Merci ! . . .—Tu viens . . .—Je vous suis." So ends the first Act.

For this suite of diverse Scenes, unified by one dominant idea—the return of Ulysses—Fauré has written music of astonishing pliancy, suppleness and truthfulness. We have seen how, in his simpler settings for voice and piano, he succeeded in preserving the unity of the rhythm and an impeccable steadiness of form, with emphasis where necessary on particular words ; the same is apparent in all these changing scenes. To the charming music of the flute players Penelope adds her plea : " Ulysses, fier époux . . ." And here, in this extended prayer, the warrior's theme, stealing in in the rhythm of the dance, becomes more and more prominent, and finally blazes out in Penelope's cry, " Help my distress ! "

To the imperious and harsh Suitors' theme, its asperity intensified by harmonies resulting from the imitations, is contrasted the weariness of Ulysses—where, in certain chords and melodic inflections, can be detected the shadow of that subtlety and cunning which had baffled the Cyclops. Penelope's accents have a matchless nobility, regal—

E

with an affectionate ardour[1] never surpassed even in *la Bonne Chanson*. In the meantime there are episodes such as he only could conceive : the dances, precise, and gracefully supple ; the grave mystery of Penelope's warning, " Les Dieux Ouraniens prennent tous les visages " ; the passionate monologue when Ulysses, alone for an instant, declaims ringingly, " Épouse chérie . . ." ; finally, the marvellous canon with which the Act closes, its double line unfolding with the perfection of a Greek bas-relief.

Second Act. Few Scenes—simple and spacious—but whose intense emotion gives them a rare intensity of life. An eminence overlooks the sea. At the rise of the curtain, in the still moonlight, a nocturne is heard : a dialogue between Eumaeus and a shepherd, over an orchestral background of serene melancholy, the harmony ceaselessly coiling and uncoiling ("neither wholly itself, nor wholly anything else," Verlaine would have said). Can we not say that Fauré himself, one evening on the shores of his beloved Mediterranean, experienced this antique pastoral, among the green oaks of the mountains, their Virgilian shadows lengthening in the sunset ? . . . Enter Penelope, followed by Euryclée ; Ulysses is with them. She recalls memories— dreams of former times, when her husband was young and still with her. There is a long Duet with the " aged stranger " ; and each rivals the other in prudence and discretion. The Queen questions him, still mistrustful : " For all around me is so much deceit, that I can trust no one at first sight." Ulysses, fertile improviser that he is, soon concocts a story : the warrior has lived under his roof, in Crete, for twelve days. To prove his tale, he describes minutely the appearance, the dress, the armour of the hero ; and, carried away by his own romancing, his tears fall . . . But his wife is uneasy : has Ulysses remained faithful ? He has not fallen a prey to the seductions of some stranger ? And here, in the heat of his reply, the wily Ulysses, the " fertile inventor," forgets his *rôle :* " Could he, whose heart has been intoxicated by thy voice, yield to the charm of any other wine ? " . . . he had " one desire only, in all that terrible exile : to feel thee swooning once more in his happy arms ! " It is impossible to describe the expressive force the music attains in this long, pathetic and sustained development depicting the memories, the future hope, which move the hero. What does it matter that the unseeing, the devotees of some kind of veristic drama, consider this not " theatre," even though it all breathes an indescribable ardour ? And, if others, the Wagnerites, have denounced the presence of a technique dear to the composer of Tristan (that of *leit-motifs*), that merely proves the technique open to all, for there is no question that it has produced music both living and personal. That of Fauré, here particularly, is of the highest order ; in perfection of writing, with a supreme control by which the feeling is never constrained— is, indeed, by the harmonious form, rendered still more intense.

Penelope is astonished : " Comme tu dis cela . . . Comme tu dis cela ! " . . . Ulysses almost discloses his identity, but recovers himself. While Eumaeus re-enters, he proposes a stratagem to his

---

[1] *Cf.* page 52, " *J'ai tant d'amour a lui donner encore. . .*"

wife : " Give yourself only to him who can bend the Bow of Ulysses "
—knowing full well that Ulysses alone has the strength ; in his hands
the weapon will consummate his vengeance. Penelope, almost in
despair, re-enters the palace. Left alone, Ulysses calls Eumaeus and
the shepherds. " Behold the most to be pitied of mortals . . . I am
Ulysses, your King ! " He implores their help ; and following this,
sure of victory, surrounded by partisans who will give their aid in
slaying the infamous wretches, his theme, triumphal, bursts forth
in the orchestra, in bold relief and with extraordinary conciseness—
a brilliant triple canon mingled with the clashing of swords, with
harmonies cruel, savage—but logical, *analysable* and, in spite of all,
*classical* . . . One thinks of the Iliad. And this pitiless victory
makes a picture all the more striking in contrast to the serene ending
of the first Act, the Nocturne in the second, and the tenderness of
the incomparable Duet.

Third Act. Scene I. An Aria (Ulysses), impetuous, violent, dark
with threats and inflamed with anger. A thundering transition, in
three chords, from G Flat Minor to D Minor, sets squarely before
us the heroic figure of Hercules, whose colossal sword Ulysses has
recognised among his armour. He hides it under the throne whereon
Penelope will sit. Scene II. The aged Eurycleia tells her master[1]
of the Queen's distress. He reassures her. The stratagem of the
Bow will make him victorious. " And to-night you will see Penelope
smile." (Here an unexpected modulation, extremely simple, a sudden
shaft of light, felicitous, charming and noble—such as the master
possessed the secret of !). Scene III. Eumaeus, rejoicing, announces
to the King that all is as he wished. By a lucky chance the shepherds
will be there, gathered for a sacrifice ordered by the Intruders :
" Thirteen sheep, twenty cows and a hundred heifers." Scene IV.
Entry of the Suitors. They summon Penelope to make her choice.
" Which of you can bend the Bow of Ulysses . . . shall remain in
the palace," she replies. But then, struck by a strange presentiment,
she implores them to renounce it. " Death is here . . . I see these
walls covered in blood and reeking entrails. The warrior returns,
he is already near . . ." The prophecy is in vain ; it seems to the
sceptics only a ruse. Each tries to bend the Bow. Each gives it up,
powerless (extraordinary music, imitative, or rather suggestive, of
this abortive effort). In his turn, Ulysses, still disguised as an old man,
wishes to have a try ; all consent, with contemptuous raillery.
Stupefaction : " He has bent the Bow—the arrow has gone through
the rings ![2] He bends the Bow again ; aiming at Eurymachus, " And
this time, *you* are the target ! " The rival falls. His vanquisher
now throws off all disguise ; he straightens himself, terrible of aspect.
The Suitors flee in terror. From then on it is a massacre. Ulysses,
Eumaeus and the shepherds throw themselves in pursuit of the
fugitives ; not one of them escapes. Re-enter the King, avenged :
" Justice is done." And the work ends with a triumphal chorus
acclaiming the happiness of the reunited couple.

---

[1] *Whom she has recognised since the first Act.*
[2] *The trial of skill was not only to bend the bow, but to send the arrow through*
" *twelve rings of axes.*" (*Tr.*)

# Gabriel Fauré

In this drama, with that creative intuition which gives *precise life* to the *décor*, the words, the action, the spirit, flagging not for an instant—with its constant richness and true variety—Gabriel Fauré proclaims himself verily a musician of the theatre. And that with no concessions, and by no elaborate devices, and by the most beautiful *symphonic style* ; thus showing the absurdity of that old nonsense of " water-tight compartments " in the palace of Music. In like manner the excuses which patched-up and tasteless works would like to put forward—the pretended " necessities of the drama," the scenic effects, to cover up the " bad places in the music "—also disappear. But the theatre is a bad place only for those resigned to its decline. It was a bad place for *Pénélope* no more than for *Pelléas et Mélisande*. It is true, this masterpiece of Fauré has not had the success of Madame Butterfly. Even at the outset, while it found some ardent supporters, and although at the first performances the public was clearly favourable, a number of composers found some " harshness " in the score which surprised them—quite in keeping with their preference for the first volume of songs. Always this inability to follow an evolution ! And the virile force, and sometimes the *Doricism* of this language disconcerted them. To-day the cause of this is realised : the professionals definitely understand ; in company with them, a select few of the public have gradually added some fervent enthusiasts to their number. If Fauré's art, no doubt, will never be popular with the musically uncultivated masses, in compensation one finds even in the most modest seats (and perhaps particularly there)—in the gallery which decided the success of *Pelléas*—fanatics confessing their love ; *Pénélope* has charmed them, just as they will take care never to miss a revival of *Pelléas*, and can savour all the merits of *Ariane et Barbe-Bleue*. In Paris among the less well-off there exists a number of *true artists*, driven into prosaic careers by the necessities of existence ; but no matter—they understand and love beautiful things ; and by supporting them, form a good part of the conditions necessary for their survival. So *Pénélope* from time to time reappears on the bills ; less often than one would wish—but enough for its memory to be preserved, and for succeeding generations to be nourished by this " body-building marrow " . . . The part of the heroine was created[1] by Mme. Lucienne Breval ; she proved more Queen than wife, notably in the last Act, when the action seemed a bit slow. Recently, at the Opéra-Comique, there have been Mme. Balguerie, with her dramatic intelligence and her superb voice, and then Mme. Croiza, displaying a great and indescribable emotion : moreover, one of the most profound interpreters of Faurian song.

These pages bring to an end the chapter devoted to the master's works. If it has kindled the desire to approach his compositions more closely, the volume will be not without value. But to complete it—and perhaps the most important part is yet to come—we must embark on a general study of his language, his sensitivity and the characteristics of his art.

---

[1] *In the part of Ulysses, M. Muratore was of the first order.*

60

# The Man And His Style

IF WE WOULD analyse precisely Fauré's technique, some technical terms are unavoidable. We use them with apologies, and will make them as few as possible.

A general survey is given by the following quotations :

" The tonality, harmony, rhythm, form, are those which Gabriel Fauré found at the beginning of his musical career ; in his hands, these ordinary things have become precious."[1]

" What, between ourselves, were the discreet and isolated temerities of *Printemps* which so scandalised the Institute, or of the *Pavane pour une Infante défunte*, compared with the methodical, rational and irrevocable liberation of Fauré's style, his profound and essential novelty, his conscious and organised enfranchisement ?[2] . . . For, make ro mistake, Fauré was no mere forerunner, a pioneer whose tracks were broadened by explorers better equipped. He was a musician who, a quarter of a century before the rest, spoke freely a prophetic language with an ease, virtuosity and elegance never surpassed."[3]

These verdicts supplement and balance each other. And the example of Fauré leads to this conclusion : that novelty can be achieved by quite ordinary means. The unexpectedness of a conglomeration of sounds in the main amounts to very little, even if the snobs and the simpletons marvel at it for a time ; moreover, it quickly disappears, ousted by the inevitable counter-fashions. The only element of value in a work is the quality of its music and its thought. The creation of new sounds may be necessary to some geniuses ;[4] in their case, they will not become obsolete. But others show themselves more subtly revolutionary. Persuasive, and without iconoclasm, they are no less innovators ; and such a one was Gabriel Fauré.

Reflecting on this question of living harmonic language, one realises that the isolated chord is but one, rather accessory, element. It is the chord *progression*, and the way in which this is brought about, and particularly its relation to the melody, to the evolution of the phrase and to the gradations of feeling, which is fundamental. The art of music, offering such a prodigious wealth of material, permits of innumerable combinations with the help of none but well known harmonies. As in chemistry the atoms can group themselves in thousands of ways, so successions of *chord-cells*[5] can form a discourse

---

[1] *Nadia Boulanger, article on Fauré's religious music*, Revue musicale, *October*, 1922.

[2] *E. Vuillermoz, "Gabriel Fauré," Revue musicale, October, 1922.*

[3] *Extract from the same article.*

[4] *So much the better, since they enrich the domain of music.*

[5] *Common chords, or 7ths.*

# Gabriel Fauré

that is admirable and sublime—or dull, banal and devoid of real existence. The analysis of the elements has little interest ; it is a question, on the contrary, of the *life* of chords in *succession*.[1]  Merely by concordant writing, Fauré is continually innovating ; and more so by the use of simple 7ths than ever H. Duparc achieved in *l'Invitation au Voyage.*

What is most striking, first of all, is that feeling for plainchant which has been manifest since his youth.  We have mentioned all that he owed to the teaching at l'École Niedermeyer, to the days when Saint-Saëns, himself perhaps influenced by the composer of *le Lac* and his ideas on the accompaniment of the liturgical melodies, was already turning towards the ancient Modes.  This was new ; for the composers of the 18th century and the first half of the 19th had forgotten the scales in use at the time of the Renaissance.[2]  This very marked preference of Fauré shows itself in the employment of certain of the Gregorian Modes.[3]  We have noted it more than once : in the *Requiem ;* in *les Roses d'Ispahan* (Il n'est plus de parfum . . .") ; and, most expressive, in that fine song, *Au Cimetière* (" A sa croix les parents pleurant . . .").[4]  It is impossible to overestimate the importance of this.  As we have pointed out, there is no question of learned and artificial reconstruction, but of a predetermined correspondence between the character of these scales and, most often, Fauré's very nature.  It is not by chance that the character of the Aeolian (A Minor with G Natural and F Natural), firm and virile, was preferred by the Greeks, or that they showed a marked antipathy for " *notes sensibles* "—whose expression seemed to them too restricted, too emphatic, one might say *too romantic*.[5]  The leading note lowered to G Natural in the key of A Minor, or suppressed in the Major Mode,[6] is often the precise inflection necessary to his thought.  However, it must not be regarded as a formula ; he himself wrote with the utmost freedom, reserving the right to pass from one mode to another : to use real leading notes as it pleased him—and most characteristically in certain passages whose nicety of execution demanded a sharpening of the Major Third on the Dominant to the Pythagorian Third.[7]

In the case of this great musician, a good deal of harmony is derived from this *Gregorian conception*.  It would take too long to go into

---

[1] *Progressions and modulations.*

[2] *With some rare exceptions, e.g., the Andante of Beethoven's fifteenth Quartet, in the Lydian Mode ; a few passages in Berlioz and Gounod ; and also a certain archaic colour, occasionally, in Hérold's* le Pré-aux-Clercs.

[3] *Especially those on A, G, D and E—which are also those of the old folk-songs of our own country (see the transcriptions of Bourgault-Ducoudray, M. Emmanuel, Vincent d'Indy, etc.*

[4] *To mention three works only, among many others.*

[5] " Note sensible "—*the Leading Note ; i.e., a* semitone *below the tonic* (Tr.)

[6] *This will be dealt with later.  There is also the leading note suppressed in the Minor, as at the end of* l'Inscription sur le sable (*from* Jardin clos).

[7] *The Major Third in just intonation is defined by the ratio 5 : 4 ; the Pythagorian Third, formed by successive fifths. C—G—D—A—E, is characterised by the ratio 27 : 16.  Its nature is essentially melodic ; but certain chords, from the quality of their expression (and following the sense of the phrase) demand it. Good instrumentalists are not deceived by it.*

detail ;[1] but it can be taken that a number of progressions dear to Fauré, and forbidden by the harmony books, are compatible with the character of plainchant.[2] Even the use of the common chord on the third of the scale, which Reber[3] held to be " non-existent " or dangerous, is charming—and therefore legitimate—in the *Sérénade* from *Shylock*, in *le Secret*, in *le Pays des Rêves*, etc. The Faurian enlargement of the *Plagal feeling* (that is to say, Cadences with the chord on the fourth degree, Fa la doh, leading to that of the Tonic, Doh mi soh, is seen in his well-known Cadence :

And this remains Gregorian in feeling since an ordinary cadence, a dominant chord (E, G Sharp, B) before the chord of A, would use a G Sharp (proceeding to the tonic A)—in place of the succession G Natural—A of the above example (notes belonging to the Aeolian scale on A). Finally, this Plagal sense, evinced by a desire to avoid an ending involving the semitonal leading-note, extends even to harmonies over a Dominant bass preceding the final Tonic chord. So we find a chord of the seventh or ninth with the third replaced by the fourth, thus :

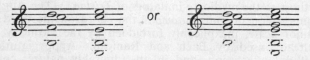

The Cadence thus acquires a remarkable quietude. In our days this is well established ; but not to resolve such a discord must have appeared scandalous in the far-off days when Fauré dared this boldness for the first time.[4]

---

[1]*See the writer's* Étude sur l'harmonie moderne, *in* l'Encyclopédie de la musique, *published by Delagrave (second part, Vol.* 1).

[2]*In C : chord of E following a chord of F ; chord of D preceded or followed by that of E ; chord of G moving to chord of F, with B-C in the top part (Cf.* Clair de lune, *in D Flat : " au calme clair de lune, triste et beau. . ."*

[3]*Reber (1807-80). From 1851 Professor of Harmony, from 1862 Professor of Composition, at the Paris Conservatoire. His* Traité d'Harmonie *was published in 1862. Koechlin would seem to be wrong on a matter of fact here ; Reber's observations concern the third degree of the Minor scale. His actual words are " Provisionally, this chord (i.e., the Augmented Triad) will be considered as impracticable or non-existent "—a cautious attitude which every teacher of elementary harmony would adopt. (Tr.)*

[4]*Nevertheless logical—and even conforming to tradition, if we extend the field of the " exceptional resolution," wherein the discordant note remains as a note of the next chord (e.g., a Dominant 7th on G followed by a first Inversion on A).*

So that, while remaining a *purist*,[1] he could seem dangerous to narrow-minded professors. After all, who was there, in the decade 1875-85, willing to recognise Gregorian tendencies? Gounod, Saint-Saëns, Lalo, Chabrier, Franck (also his disciples, Duparc, Vincent d'Indy, etc.), and on the other hand, the liberal Bourgault-Ducoudray, so enthusiastic over the Greek modes. Perhaps also Massenet, possessed of greater breadth of view than his colleagues (cf. certain chords in the Saint-Sulpice Act, of *Manon*). But the rest—to begin with Debussy (before he heard Palestrina and Orlando di Lassus, in Rome) —their culture was firmly based on leading-notes and the Dominant 7th. With Fauré the result was never that the sense of tonality became *vague.* If he achieved " vagueness " it was with precision, and knowing perfectly well the direction of the phrase. If this at times seemed to lose itself in mysterious undergrowth, the compass directions were never ignored. But the tonality, if clear-cut, was sometimes established very rapidly, and often transitorily—as we see in the 16th century, favoured by the use of the old Modes which permit great suppleness of modulation.[2] We note, too, subtle false relations, bold, but logical to the ear—such as we find in many a Bach Chorale, or in the Fugue, for string quartet, by Mozart. In this connection see the *Offertoire* from the *Requiem* (page 18, 1st and 2nd lines).

Fauré's harmonic style includes a large number of progressions little known before his time. In general, he discovered them ; sometimes he made them his own by a treatment so appropriate to the feeling and so felicitous that they became personal to him. The elements, apart from common chords, are scarcely more than different kinds of 7ths, sometimes of 9ths, with few complicated " alterations,"— he leaves those to the mediocre imitators of *Tristan*.[3] The Augmented Fifth is quite frequent, but *diatonic* :[4] the chord on the third degree of the Minor Scale, inexplicably forbidden by the harmony books, though already used by Bach and Rameau. Appoggiaturas—but always without affectation, and in an admirably natural context— aim at underlining the expression. We must also remark on his

---

[1]*We shall presently go into this question of purity in writing, as opposed to the scholastic precepts of the harmony treatises. It is not easy, without actually hearing the music and without considerable development (beyond the scope of this book) to explain the possibility of a style really pure, which nevertheless is full of licences from the point of view of the " rules." But in a word, it can be said that the text-book rules, valuable in the academy, are most conventional ; that the best musical stylists are constantly infringing them ; in fact, they are neither sufficient, nor necessary. Moreover, the boldest revolutionaries, with very few exceptions, have begun by submitting to their discipline.*

[2]*And Fauré's Gregorian education, we may be sure, developed in him that faculty of slipping gracefully and subtly from one key to another. Traces of this can be found as far back as* la Bonne Chanson. *Sometimes too the modulation is only apparent ; thus, at the beginning of the fourth Chorus of* Caligula, *the D Flat does not contradict the key of E Flat : it is really the Mixolydian Scale (key of G Major with F Natural for the seventh note.)*

[3]*Some refined " alterations " are, however, to be found in* Soir ; *the principle is based on the Dominant 7th with the Diminished 5th. (In French text-books " les altérations " designate any chromatic inflections of the notes of a chord.—Tr.)*

[4]*That is to say, it is never, save for some rare exceptions, derived from the Whole Tone Scale.*

deliberate use of Inversions ; in particular he removed the absurd suspicion which weighed upon the Second Inversion. At the time when Reber's treatise specified them as " rare," Fauré was already using them.[1]

In the handling of this technique, licences—from the standpoint of the scholastic rules—were numerous. Certainly, during his studies at l'École, he submitted to the accepted discipline, without which no one can acquire mastery. His style may be free but, on the other hand, one can think of no greater purity. But do not compare the precepts of harmony books and grammars ; the tradition of the most illustrious and most truly *pure* masters (notably Bach and Mozart) is to infringe on each page, *almost on each line*, the " laws " relating to direct 5ths and 8ves, false relations, etc. With Gabriel Fauré had become legitimate, and henceforward classic, the following licences : 7ths prepared or resolved by transference ; unprepared 7ths (even on the 1st and 4th degrees of the scale, i.e., Major 7ths) ; a rising bass, in a chord of the Tritone or the 2nd ; chromatic false relations ; appoggiaturas irregularly resolved, etc. As for the " exceptional resolutions " in *le Ruisseau*, the *Requiem, Madrigal*, you will find them charming ; *Nell, les Roses d'Ispahan, la Fée aux Chansons, la Rose*, and a great many other songs, show many essentially Faurian traits which have passed into current language.[2] In all this, Fauré's *rôle* as forerunner is clear—as defined so well by M. Emile Vuillermoz. Any more considerable development of the question would be in place only in a harmony treatise ; we must confine ourselves to a few questions from his works. (See following page.)

Although he achieved a homogeneous synthesis of all musical technique, it is necessary for the purpose of analysis to divide our studies : after Harmony, Counterpoint. This is admirably balanced in character, with marked independence (after the style of Bach), in absolute respect for the harmony (that is to say, the quality of the aggregation of sounds simultaneously perceived by the ear). As an organist, a pupil of Saint-Saëns and a fervent admirer of John Sebastian, he would naturally be inspired by the technique of the great Cantor. Notice already, towards the end of the *Offertoire*, the broad and smooth working out of the three-part canon, " O Domine." The logical movement of parts is found again, with a boldness even more Bach-like, in *la Bonne Chanson* (cf. *Une Sainte en son auréole*, 16th and 17th bars) ; in several bars of *Mandoline ;* in *Prométhée* (the Prelude, chorus, and scene with Bia and Kratos, from the first Act ; Pandora's funeral procession, etc.). At about the time of the *Requiem* (1888) a few musicians had revived the style

---

[1] *Or, in any case, very soon after this time.*

[2] *The consecutive 7ths in* au Bord de l'eau *are carried out with infinite grace ; their audacity remains unnoticed, but in their day it was great.* Prison *contains two consecutive 9ths : but Fauré has expressly stated that, to his ear this actual " parallel" implies a crossing of the inner parts, with contrary motion chancing to correct what perhaps he thought was of too free and " facile " a style. This, moreover, was before* Pelléas, *but after Chabrier's* le Roi malgré lui (1886-7), *in which can be found an admirably clear example of a similar progression (Duet between Alexina and Henri de Valois). Later (cf. Prelude in F) Fauré wrote parallel progressions without scruple.*

# Gabriel Fauré

Echangent des pro-pos fa - des sous    les ra - mu - - res

(a) Unprepared 7th.                                "Mandoline"

Par de - là l'heure hu - maine    et le temps in - fi - ni

Chromatic false relation.                          "Le Parfum
                                                   Impérissable."

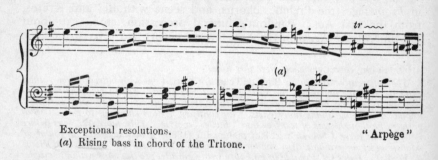

Exceptional resolutions.
(a) Rising bass in chord of the Tritone.            "Arpège"

Exceptional resolution.  " Nocturne "

False relation of the Tritone.  " Clair de Lune "

Irregular resolution.  " Chanson "

# Gabriel Fauré

of Bach,—Saint-Saëns, and particularly Bizet (cf. *l'Arlésienne*, and *Carmen*, with their bold clashes). In this matter then, you may say that Fauré was not absolutely a pioneer, though much in advance of the greater part of his contemporaries. But—apart from the personal flavour of his contrapuntal harmony—his bold passing-notes were brought about with a marvellous feeling for fulness and harmonic quality; a rare feat which demanded a remarkable taste.[1] And, as with Bach and Mozart, the success is most particularly notable when the theme is in the lower part. Then the difficulty is immensely increased, since this lower part, though predetermined, must always make a *good bass*. Fauré enjoyed such a constraint; indeed, it only stimulated his imagination. But with him—because counterpoint was never an obstacle to his perfect musicianship—the Bass was of prime importance. And here a word to pianists: he never ceased to advocate this necessary support, too often neglected by virtuosi to the point of leaving in mid-air, suspended in the void, a melody thus deprived of all harmonic sense.

The fugal style was never distasteful to him. He had never the narrow-mindedness which condemns a tradition as being scholastic. He restored to life these methods of former times. Re-read the *Requiem, Dolly*, the second Violin Sonata, for smoothly-worked canons; and particularly, in *Pénélope*, the last page of the first Act, as well as the thundering imitations (on the Ulysses theme) at the end of the second.[2] The fugal entries, or rather free imitations (the Suitors' theme, in *Pénélope*; the second subject of the first Piano Quartet; the passage for strings only, in the second Quintet; etc.), will completely convince you that he was right. *Over*-intellectual he was never; what was allowable in this style becomes over-intellectual only to those incapable of realising its sensitive beauty.

To return to the realm of harmony, with the study of his Modulations. They aroused the critics. Lenepveu could not stomach the progression, so beautiful and expressive, and so *essential*, by which the primary key is reached at the cadence of the first phrase of *le Parfum impérissable*. Another professor could not understand, and has never understood; it is too late now for him ever to understand. Besides, one only grasps the sense of these subtle transitions by musicianship and deep feeling. The logic of an elementary analysis, and even the logic of the practice of the eighteenth century " classics," are here seen to be quite erroneous. Thus, in *Nell*: being in a key

---

[1] *Despite the theoretical independence of the parts, they were never forced into unnecessary dissonance, nor poor or platitudinous harmony; horizontal movement could never forget vertical.*

[2] *One could quote many other examples, notably the Adagio from the first Quintet, the* Fantaisie *for Piano and Orchestra, the later Nocturnes, etc. The use of " échappées," and especially ascending retardations, furnished the occasions for all kinds of new effects, often very daring, the clashes very dissonant—but always apposite and to the point. (An anticipation is already seen in the syncopated counterpoint in the First Nocturne, at the return of the initial theme.) This study is most fascinating for the student; it is naturally beyond the scope of this work.*

*Note.*—" *Echappée—an irregular resolution of Passing Notes. Most of the examples quoted in Reber are either elisions or developments of the Nota Cambiata formula.* (Tr.)

(D Flat) nearly related to the main key (G Flat), before the return
to this key why not a modulation to F Major, this giving oneself
the pleasure of an unexpected, but thoroughly musical, reappearance?
A parallel " illogicality " (though profoundly logical) appears at the
end of the Tenor Aria in the first Act of *Prométhée* : in order to
finish in C—already reached—he plunges into F, on a 6/4 chord ;
the incomparable brilliancy of the peroration being due to the return
to the *preceding, but almost forgotten,* tonality.  One could easily
multiply these examples ;  we will mention only the final cadence of
*Puisque l'aube grandit* (*la Bonne Chanson*).  Try setting the words,
" Je ne veux pas d'autre paradis " with a progression which does
not modulate, and see the result !  The sense demands this paradoxical,
but necessary and exact " fancy " :  the supple, ingenuous, translucent
modulation from F to G Major.  Thus, the relationship of keys
springs from a legitimate cause, expressive and musical :  it is the
very essence of the idea, and never empty trifling with ingenious
scintillation, as it were " shot silk," as was thought by those who
have never grasped the logic of this art.  As for its realisation, it is
matchlessly easy and assured.[1]  The simplicity of his methods should
be noted, preserving the excellent *naïveté* of writing that he loved.
Thus, at the end of *C'est l'extase*, a perfect cadence brings to a close
this exquisite and profound song ;  in *Prométhée*, he is not afraid
of the obsolescent (?) 6/4, to be found also at the conclusion of the
first song in *la Bonne Chanson* (*Une Sainte en son auréole*).  We shall
return later to the question of Fauré's simplicity ;  refinement does
not prevent simplicity, and simplicity is no bar to refinement.

As for the question of Form, this seems too complex to study
without even reading the music.  The general plan (ternary) conforms
to that of the Allegro movements of Beethoven and Mozart.  The
function of the Sequence is not despised [2] an old technique which,
however, he took care not to turn into a " Rosalia."  Sometimes
the tonality will be found established over long periods, with no
modulation ;  then, the fundamental bars first heard will be repeated
at the 2nd or 3rd.[3]  This modulatory life keeps up the interest with
rich and compact harmonies ;  the symmetry remains supple—ordered,
but obeying no merely geometrical instinct.  The same suppleness is
found in Concertante style, with the different parts answering each
other.  Re-read, too (cf. the Chapter on the Chamber Music) the
quotations from our worthy colleague M. Vuillermoz ;  there is no
one better calculated to make clear the independence the composer
could preserve in the traditional framework he imposed on himself.

Finally, touching the instrumentation, we have already remarked
on its principal characteristics.  Moreover, *Dolly* was scored by

---

[1] *It would be too long and technical to study all his methods.  We must, however,
mention the use of " pivot chords "—that is to say, a modulation produced by the
ambiguity of one chord belonging to two different keys (usually a common chord or
6th).  The Supertonic 7th is also a great resource, as often with Bizet (in quite a different sense) :  it leads with the utmost precision to the Dominant chord, or one of its
inversions (cf. Prelude to* Pelléas et Mélisande).

[2] *And particularly in his later works, in which many periods of 2 and 4 bars are thus
repeated.  Their beauty permits of such repetitions—impossible with mediocre ideas.*
[3] *Cf. the first Chorus of* Prométhée :  " Eia eia. . . ."

M. Rabaud ; it is not certain that the orchestral version of *Caligula*
was by Fauré ; *Pelléas et Mélisande* was confided to the present
writer ; *Prométhée* to the Director of Music, M. Eustace ; *Pénélope*
in part (to all appearances) to one of his friends—whether d'Indy
or Paul Dukas I know not, and the secret has been well kept.
Sometimes his doublings of Strings and Wood-wind go some way
towards diminishing the total effect (as in *la Naissance de Vénus*).
But since for him this side of his art was somewhat accessory, and
as most often one cannot state definitely that he was responsible for
the orchestration, it is better to refrain from criticisms or eulogies
which may not be his due.

The study of this Faurian technique shows what will be discussed
again in due course : his freedom with regard to the fashions of
his time. He always remained himself, without departing from
traditional ways (understanding by this the best, those of Bach). Was
he influenced by Wagner's ninths ? Impossible to say ; but he need
not have been. The chord was well known ; and besides he used
it in his own quite personal way. If on the other hand, in that
beautiful appoggiatura, " J'aurais pitié du coeur des hommes,"[1] Claude
Debussy seems to have led Fauré towards a parallel path (cf. *la Forêt
de Septembre, le Don silencieux*—same harmony—and equally in the
second Quintet, as well as in *Pénélope :* " Tu pleures . . ." p. 145),
it is of no importance—and no one would dream of speaking of
reminiscence. Everything that the master obtained by this means[2]
was personal to him. But one should not be too unmindful of all
this ; to use correctly, and with beauty, chords that have inspired
you in other musicians' hands, needs not less talent than to write
chords entirely new. Perhaps it needs more.

Technical study, necessary to any serious monograph, remains
specialised however, and can give only a vague idea of the physiognomy
or the sensitiveness of the artist. Only by hearing the music can you
grasp the bond between the sounds we have just analysed, and the
expression—the state of soul (conscious or not) anterior to the production of the work. What we are attempting in this book is to prepare
for this, by describing the " inmost soul " as it is apparent in his
compositions, so far as we have been able to recognise it ; after which
certain general characteristics of his art will present a sort of synthesis.

Fauré's evolution preserves sufficient unity[3] for it to be traced only
in broad outlines. It is the story of the unfolding of his individuality
to the point where it displays itself in the most profound and striking
manner. Gradually the foreign influences, the parasitical excrescences
engendered by a literature that did not suit him, became assimilated.
(Thus appear to us *Rêve d'amour*, or *les Djinns*, by Victor Hugo.)
It took him some time to eliminate the dross ; it is noticeable in
*Fleur jetée* and perhaps even in *Poème d'un jour*. With the *musical*

---

[1] *Pelléas et Mélisande, page 219 (2nd Edition) (Arkel's phrase).*

[2] *As Debussy, for his part, took the 9ths of Erik Satie (Sarabandes 1887), and as
Wagner, certain discoveries of Liszt : for example, the chorus of Brunnhilde's slumber,
which we are assured were borrowed from the Faust Symphony.*

[3] *Despite the " three periods " we have particularised above—in the chapter devoted
to his piano works.*

influences it is quite otherwise ; with a persistent suppleness they were turned in the direction of his own domain, enriched by passing detours. He was led to the discovery of his own personality by certain poems : first, those, lyrical in form, which satisfied a feeling for nature (*Chant d'Automne*, Baudelaire), or else his innate love of Venice[1] and for the Italy of Frescobaldi and the Florentine painters.[2] Often too he couples with it a sensitivity washed by the broad current of romanticism. Besides the purely musical considerations[3] you see therefore that it is poetry, or travel—real or imaginary—or the orientation due to the subject (*Prométhée*), and particularly the *inner* evolution (towards that serenity, alternating with anguish, of his last years), that are the stages on the road leading to his real self, until he obtained complete self-expression and from then on attempted only what was profoundly true. In short, we find ourselves led to the study of the Man.

In the Chapter on his Life we drew a rapid sketch of his appearance. It is difficult to picture him without that halo of white hair, as we have known him for so many long years. To see him as he was as a young man we must turn to his eldest son, M. Emmanuel Fauré-Frémiet—the very picture, it seems. There is the same delicacy, that " breeding " whose distinction clothes the apparent tranquillity of an Eastern sage—and a certain smile, not entirely free from irony—but below the surface, and never turning to bitterness. His look was strangely distant, as his eyes followed the smoke of the eternal cigarette. But study the fine sketch, by Sargent, done in London about 1898, at the time of the performances of *Pelléas et Mélisande* ; here you can see the energy, hidden under an air of nonchalance. We would have loved to see him some day in Arab costume, as it were the descendant of one of those delightful poets of old, such as we meet in M. Klingsor's poems and M. Franz Toussaint's translations. But he never indulged in such whims—even shunning with care a Bohemian appearance. No one was simper in dress : not " smart," but always correct ; neither " starchy " nor casual.

As for his real self, his connection with *le Figaro* shows him in his relations with his colleagues and society. He was above all benign and courteous ; an example by which, if they were capable, the pretentious incompetents who think they know everything (or would like to seem so), ceaselessly searching for the faults of a work, might profit. To say or to write unpleasant things was repugnant to him, as much by reason of his natural good-nature as that modesty which characterised him. And with Massenet, and Puccini, when he recognised *music* in certain pages it was *he*, emphatically, who was right—a wiser attitude than the contempt of the snobs. His dedication of *le Parfum impérissable* to Paolo Tosti, composer of trashy ballads, was not, as might be supposed, irony, biting and cynical (and vain), but a souvenir of pleasant relations without measuring the gulf separating them.

---

[1] Barcarolle, Shylock.
[2] Sérénade toscane, Clair de lune.
[3] *The influence of Bach, Mendelssohn, Chopin, Gounod—and Saint-Saëns, whom it would be unjust to forget.*

# Gabriel Fauré

If one adds that <u>he was not</u> essentially literary-minded, nor philosophical in conversation or writing, certain reservations are necessary. He had a deep affection for the poets. Capable of conceiving abstract ideas, he did not dissociate himself from philosophical problems (particularly touching the arts). But he never practised dialectic after the current fashion. His bent was not that of a Leonardo da Vinci, the explicit knowledge of phenomena ; the search for causes formed no part of the depth of his mind. He spent no time in analysing. He saw the world, primarily, as a mine of *harmony* ; impressions vividly experienced, his work determined by a state of mind—a synthesis of which he was profoundly conscious. Moreover, he was interested in this searching for causes, this analysis, in other people ; often he would find developed there themes dear to him.[1]  If he reserved his best leisure, not for the study of M. Bergeret, but for the transports of poetry or the countryside, transforming them into music, his was not the worse choice.

His articles show no virtuosity of style, no striving after effect ; on the contrary, no one was further removed from rhetoric. He put forward his views with no elaborate phraseology ; soberly, clearly and exactly. But it is certain that he felt more deeply than his words show, the art of music being his medium. While life allowed him, he sang of life, with a sort of recognition of having loved beauty, with that singular optimism, that intimate happiness which carried in itself the gift of being made manifest in music. As with all artists of lively sensibility, the reality was inferior to his dream, but nevertheless fine and wonderfully healthy.

At present we are, perhaps, attempting the impossible, by trying to put Fauré's sensibility into words.

It is both charming and forcible. Opposite poles : too often one sees only the first. But the balance of his art is held delicately : in his technique, original discipline and freedom ; in his soul, that mixture of tenderness and inner energy (although a certain willpower was lacking, in that he did not always know how to refuse) ; finally, in his general aesthetic, that essentially Greek equilibrium between feeling and logic.

*The Faurian charm :* let us do away with this equivocation. When a piece of music is *musical*, and also possesses the attraction of a great success, certain cross-grained people affect to believe that it is no more than an ear-tickling appeal to the senses. Thus, the detractors of Gounod's *Faust*. Happily, this contempt seems to be going out of fashion ; but it was formidable and unwholesome at the time of the Wagner idolatry. But the charm of Fauré—and often of Gounod—penetrates deeper than mere sensation. To be sure, it is not, in origin, free from sensuousness. This is necessary to every artist ; sensual response to the beauty of chord and line, to nature, to beauty in all its forms—for example, feminine beauty.[2]

[1] *It has been shown in a previous quotation (cf the Chapter on the Piano Works) that he was not incapable of expressing these things himself—and sometimes, not without beauty.*

[2] *Though this general sensuousness extends to many subjects other than that studied by Freud, to which some people would reduce all kinds of pleasure—a very debatable proposition !*

72

But what then? Does not art rely on matter? And is not matter the primordial condition, the mainstay of all expression that has been brought to fruition? With Debussy, and with Mozart, you will find a like attractiveness of the " substantial," without blame being attached to it[1] because this substance is quickened by the inner life of the human spirit. I would not say, moreover, that an analogous charm is not found in Bach, in the luxuriance of his chords, or in the ornamentations of his modulations, which have nothing of a dry intellectualism. And this *sensuousness* of Bach, Mozart, Fauré and Debussy does not preclude a pure style of writing, *constructional ability*, or the *power of evoking the profoundest thoughts*.

If one returns to the man himself, one finds a thoughtful seriousness alternating with an amiable and almost childlike playfulness.[2] A child he always remained—in the best sense of the word : laughing heartily at a joke, without unkindness or bad taste—amusing himself like a little boy with a *Quadrille tétralogique* (an unpublished work, after Wagner), which he played in duet form with his good friend André Messager.

And that shows us the *complete simplicity of his soul*. People are mistaken with regard to the nature of the Faurian refinement. The writer of the *Berceuse*, from *Dolly*, and *la Fileuse*, from *Pelléas*, possessed from the very first that *naïveté*, the result of his individuality, from his having something to say—from his " ideas."[3] These he then developed with no care for effect—a great source of strength. Never did he fear the simplicity of quite ordinary harmonies (it is needless to return to the examples quoted, perfect cadences and 6/4's). To grasp the full import of this, modify the final line of *C'est l'extase* with, say, some pretentious appoggiatura (E Natural—F), or a suspension in the manner of M. Reynaldo Hahn (E Flat—D Flat), and you will see at once how Fauré remains audaciously simple.[4] Writing this, we are reminded of the learned ignoramus who talked to us of the " over-elaborate " themes which, as Director of the Conservatoire, Fauré submitted for the fugue competition ! Nothing, on the contrary, could be clearer than these themes[5]—so tuneful, and free of all false chromaticism.

In his case the refinement *never* sprang from the desire for distinction, the fear of being banal ; and on the other hand he condescends to the most familiar chords with the most perfect good grace. His refinement is the expression of the idea. The depth and intensity of the phrase often demands those modulatory gradations,[6] in which he never lost his way—and those unexpected cadences leading him back to the principal key.[7] Fauré's simplicity is Verlaine's : " Au

---

[1] *On the contrary, it is rather the primary duty of the artist.*

[2] *As the* Theme and Variations *following his* Valses-Caprices.

[3] *The action was reciprocal : the musical idea benefited by the anterior simplicity.*

[4] *The audacity is unpremeditated and unconscious ; but he could act in no other way, obedient to the perfect taste of his musical instinct, in keeping moreover with the profundity of his nature.*

[5] *As well as his very beautiful Chorales, for the counterpoint Prize.*

[6] *Cf.* Dans la Nymphée, *from* le Jardin clos.

[7] *Cf.* Le Parfum impérissable : " *On peut l'épandre toute.*"

*calme* clair de lune—triste et *beau . . .*" It is simple and refined by turns ; or rather, it is both at once, for its refinement remains as simple as the imperceptible curves in the Parthenon, as the slightly modified dimensions of its columns. And so it is always with great artists ; study the harmony of Bach's fugues or chorales.

Besides, to consider only the nature more or less complex of a chord or progression is an elementary method, and susceptible of error ; analysis will reveal *complexities* whose effect is *simple*, because they embody that absolute perfection, that logic where nothing is useless, that ease thanks to which the whole thing proceeds without a stop, with no faltering—phrase and harmony going exactly to their appointed place.

This charm, developing from the youthful affability of *l'Aubade*, and moving—with a thousand successive and variegated evolutions —towards the inner melancholy of *Clair de lune*, or that, more explicit, of *Spleen*, culminating at last in *la Chanson d'Ève* and *l'Horizon chimérique*—is founded on goodness, tenderness and love. Before all things this music is *loving*. It never mocks or sneers, never makes its way by caricature.[1] It is varied by the thousand sentiments touching love. Sometimes it is seen as proceeding from pure and sensitive sound, as in the joyous finale of *la Bonne Chanson*—and that to the first Act of *Prométhée*, where the master approaches to the passionate exaltation of Bach.[2] But often, too, it is the intimate mingling of a hidden melancholy with a certain serenity. Sometimes, again (more rarely, it is true) one is aware of a stormy night, with dark eddies on the sea. Grief is not far from this essentially human work[3]—nor even (though exceptionally), anger ; look again at the D Minor *Prélude*. It is necessary to survey the whole gamut : from the vibrant good humour of *la Bonne Chanson*, the noble ardour of *Pénélope*, to the " open wound " and serene forgiveness of *le Parfum impérissable*—from the " adolescence " of *Aubade*, *Nell*, *Aurore*, to the maturity of *la Forêt de Septembre*, then to the youthfulness, as imagined and recreated, of the incomparable *Danseuse* (from *Mirages*) —or the Scherzo of the second Quintet—this work finishing with the hidden farewell that the String Quartet conceals.

Impossible to classify, to confine within limits, a sensitivity so diverse —and nevertheless, so wholly *one ;* any two bars of Fauré are his and no one else's. But the human heart is a world in itself which this seer has explored to the furthermost corners, the most grief-laden depths, as well as describing its most obvious and naïvely ingenuous aspects. He enters at last the serene sanctuary, the haven of rest[4] after so many storms : a serenity sometimes deceptive : born of

---

[1]*Apart from the good-humoured jest of the* Quadrille tétralogique, *which did not preclude a lively admiration for Wagner.*

[2]*Cf. the Aria from the Pentecost Cantata ; the Resurrexit, from the B Minor Mass, etc.*

[3]*Élégie, for Cello ; the* Requiem, Spleen, Prison, *etc.*

[4]*It is scarcely necessary to refute certain criticisms, tending to the conclusion that this serenity " lacks emotion " : that it is perfect, but " ne faisant point pleurer." This shows a lack of comprehension of Fauré's art, similar to that suffered formerly among such aestheticians, by Greek art. We shall return to this later.*

many a previous suffering, the scar not always healed. Do we not find among the unfathomable Chorales of Bach something of the same nature? Thus we come to the end of the road leading to the heart's depths, to " cet ami sublime que tu as en toi " (Baghavâd Gitâ).

And the power of this sweet and penetrating charm is already very great : to the point where it would not require much more for the musical and *sensitive* attraction of *le Parfum impérissable* to become, itself, an intense *force*. But dynamism properly so-called—rhythm—and solid weightiness, and even a certain brutal energy were never lacking in Gabriel Fauré. To be sure, this is not an art of fisticuffs ; his music is not pugilistic. When it does achieve violence[1] order and harmony are present too ; it thus becomes all the more striking. In certain cases the power is vivid and undeniable, and it is amazing that everyone has not yet recognised it ; as for example the first Act and final chorus of *Prométhée*. There is realised in music, with the most superb *élan*, the very phrase of that enthusiastic salutation, " Prométhée est la *Force* ! " But this Force sometimes appears under a different aspect. Thus, the tranquil and expressive austerity of the deep meditation with which the 7th Nocturne (in C Sharp Minor) opens. A dynamic action is there as it were latent—because of the *weight* of this music, heightening in the extreme the effect of the combination of " movement " with " mass "—a deep sea wave, quite the opposite to a breaker, impotent and dispersed in spray. This inner but irresistible *potential* is found in Bach ; a contrast to the efforts, often successful, of emotional wrestlers—in another style.

The relationship of the material to feeling is scarcely analysable ; but it may be permitted to point out the appropriateness of the technique ; notably those inescapable passing-notes—tranquil, indispensable, their progress interrupted by nothing whatever. *Prométhée*, like the Bach fugues, makes full use of them : first in the Prelude, then in the first Chorus ; later, in the scene with Bia and Kratos, " c'est dans la solitude effroyable . . ." ; and we must also mention, among so many other examples, the triple canon at the end of the second Act of *Pénélope*.

It may be that the ease with which these are realised has deceived people.[2] No doubt, to certain semi-civilised understandings, " vitriol " is needed before an art becomes " powerful."[3] People have felt, perhaps, because of this clear, logical and perfect musicianship, that it was less strong than many more strident works—a disputable point. But also, while people have not learnt to appreciate this severe strength, wherein asperity preserves a charm, they ignore it. Few musicians

---

[1]*Cf.* Fleur jetée, *or the invective of Bia and Kratos in* Prométhée, *or of the Suitors in* Pénélope—*or, again, the anger of the D Minor* Prélude.

[2]*And even, is not the deceptive nonchalance of certain works but the outward and visible sign of an order which has bound the whole into most perfect harmony ?*

[3]*This implies no depreciation of polytonal, or even atonal, music. The writer of this book has had recourse too often to these means to be suspected of ill-feeling towards the style of Stravinsky or Schönberg. But it is true of polytonality as of language, according to Aesop : that its worth is as varied as the worth of those who use it.*

# Gabriel Fauré

know *Prométhée*. The last *Nocturnes*, the first Quintet and many powerful songs are rarely performed ; those who see in Fauré nothing but slender inspiration hold an erroneous view that all " informed criticism " would deem obsolete.

In actual fact, they are ignorant because they do not understand, and do not want to understand ; because to Grecian (or simply French) beauty, which has few initiates, they prefer something with grosser contrasts, or stupid ornamentation. Which leads us to a study of the Hellenic nature of his art, as well as the reasons why some people remain estranged from the great master.

It is advisable, first of all, to clarify matters. Granted that the subject of Prometheus, and the closer view of Aeschylus thus obtained, were determining factors in this orientation—yet it was a question less of *subject* or local colour, than of more inward things ; for *la Chanson d'Ève* and the second Quintet are as Greek as *l'Inscription sur le sable, Danseuse* or *Pénélope*.

Conciseness, clearness, choice of technique . . . Athenian clarity in an art which has been likened to " shot silk " : but one had only to hear Fauré at the piano to grasp that a strict style did not preclude nuance of expression ; to realise that the melodic line in *Arpège* or *Mandoline* remained precise, with a winged fancy, a dreamy sensitivity, and that background, sometimes, of an almost unreal past. And always there is the paradox—incomprehensible to grosser minds—of clarity of form and ease, of solidarity and suppleness, of superficial nonchalance and latent energy. Thus Fauré's charm remains Doric— Ionic often—and never inclines to the Corinthian.

All these qualities of reserve, of tact, contribute to the *force* of an art persuasive and serene, quite opposed to that of those athletes of Herculean build, with veins distended in the effort towards the sublime. With Fauré there is none of that muscular effort of the *Last Judgment*, no pathos of the Laocoon type, but the perfect, pure and complete strength—effortless and unobtrusive—of a beautiful antique torso.[1] And, as we have just pointed out, this force has indeed some *inner* life, which renders it more powerful than many a violent progression. *There is no striving after effect.* When the blow does fall, the striking power is in perfect proportion. The harmony, compact with music, charged with emotion, is " dense " ; and this human *density* endows the elements of this language with *mass*, just as in the atom the ions are animated by electricity, the resulting vortex giving the notion of weight.

Also, one will never find " pure movement," movement for movement's sake, the rhythms beating in the void because the thought is non-existent.[2] The force is from within ; virtual, potential, in all

---

[1]*He lapses but rarely, if ever, into a " neo-Greek style à la Saint-Saëns," wherein the idea and the sensibility are not sustained as well as one could wish. Moreover, Saint-Saëns by no means always displayed this frigidity, which has been much exaggerated.*

[2]*The objection may be raised, that a* beauty of pure percussion *is possible ; for instance, the end of Stravinsky's* l'Histoire du soldat. *But first, there is the question, here, of contrast with the vocal portions ; and secondly, this art foreign to musical* sounds (*for it makes use of intensities, duration, and loudness of* noises *only) has nothing to fear from the platitudes of melody and harmony to which we allude.*

the beauty of the idea.[1] And this again is very Grecian, in the harmoniousness of this invincible force. The Prelude to *Prométhée* gives us a moving picture of sonorous waves, suggesting the billows of the ocean ; and likewise, that great surge of grief which rises, swells and unfurls itself so nobly in Pandora's funeral ceremony.[2]

All that is ordered, assured, and logical in the support which such a mass can contribute to the spring of the rhythmic urge, Fauré shows equally by his balance of charm and reason : the discreet propriety of all this, proportionate to the figure and nature of Man—what could be more Greek ? Here are no deformities or romantic excesses ; not only no grotesque ugliness, but no impossible desires, no irremediable despair[3]—even in the *Nocturnes*, no " cosmic visions," no gigantic Milky Ways[4] ; only perfect and serene grandeur (second Act of *Pénélope*), limited to the human—Mediterranean—horizon.[5] To be sure, this Romanticism to which we have alluded may be capable of real beauty ; it can produce a certain sublimity. And doubtless, if one accepts this extension to extra-human or supernatural boundaries, the disproportion exists no longer ; if that is granted, there is harmony in the emotion of this pathos seeking the infinite. But conceptions of this kind, smacking rather of the North (and which appertain even more to the Gothic—or more still, to that paganism of prehistoric Russia, with *le Sacre de Printemps*), remain as far removed from Greek as from Faurian art. Besides, if it is a question of infinity, it can be maintained that the immensity of love in the realm of the heart need concede nothing to ultra-terrestial dreams under the stars. Thus, the profundity of *le Parfum impérissable ;* thus, the image of eternity which, by means so astonishingly simple, is evoked by those last bars of *l'Inscription sur le sable*, where Death is portrayed as essentially Greek. A disciple of Einstein would write, " It is not an impression of limitlessness that emerges—however, infinitude is not absent." Space as vast as one could wish—but it remains human. It harmonises with our life.

We would add that the art of Gabriel Fauré shows itself Greek and pagan in the primordial importance it attaches to this human life. It is constantly seen : in the hymns to love which form a good portion of the composition of his second period ; in the pantheistic mysticism of *la Chanson d'Ève* or *le Jardin clos* (in close sympathy with the thought of the poet Van Lerberghe, the author of *Pan*) ; in such evocations of light and antique grace as *la Rose*, *Danseuse*, etc. ; in the passion which comes to life again in the Andante of the second

---

[1]*As with Bach : the return of a theme, well harmonised and suitably timed, will have a latent power superior, perhaps, to a pathos more directly theatrical.*

[2]*Here, the* actual *intensity is of little consequence, going simply from* p *to* mf. *This power has not always the need for* ff.

[3]*Save sometimes in his last* Nocturnes.

[4]*With the exception of the " twinkling stars " which the middle portion of the 6th* Nocturne *probably evokes ; and even here it is only the accompaniment to the melody.*

[5]*The Faurian conception of infinity will be dealt with in due course. Sometimes his " human horizon " is extremely vast, especially when the sea is in question (cf.* le Lamento, *in the first collection of songs, and even the* Barcarolle *;* au Cimetière, *in the second volume ;* Je me poserai sur ton cœur, *from* le Jardin clos).

# Gabriel Fauré

Quintet, right up to the despair of the 13th Nocturne, telling of the approaching end (this picture of death is quite different from those given by *Spleen, au Cimetière,* or even by the *Elegy* and the *Requiem,* works wherein one senses an artist far from the end of his life). The intense serenity evinced by the first movement of the second Quintet and the songs of his " third style " (*l'Inscription sur le sable ; O mort, poussière d'étoiles* . . .) is not strictly Christian in character. It is not a question of the life to come—the *In Paradisum* being moreover an exception required by the nature of the *Requiem.* Nor is it a question of the doctrine of Christianity ; and this serenity, more philosophical than dogmatic, is very different from that affirmed by Bach at the end of the *Actus Tragicus* (" To-day shalt thou be with me in Paradise ") When it does overcome the anguish of a future dimly seen (and there is beauty in this strength of mind), a certain confidence is perceived, in spite of everything, confidence in Him who has created beauty, and hope that " life will continue." We can imagine we hear, through the profound voice of music, the confession of a spiritual Athenian, for whom the soft skies, and the charm of the Mediterranean light, and the feeling of having heard the " inner God," remain for ever the essential realities. Philosophers, artists, thinkers, all striving to obey the voice of this inner conscience—none, I know, will boast (if he is sincere) of having attained a superhuman goal ; I mean, of having made all his acts correspond to his high ideal. But with them this ideal none the less exists. Fauré never posed as a moralist ; he never adopted the overweening Pharisaical attitude towards any one. But the " still, small voice " sings in his work ; he puts the best of himself into it : the dictates of his conscience are translated into his human language with all the beauty of which he was capable. All praise to the artist who has devoted his life to so full and complete a consummation of this beauty.

Such an art, supremely *civilised,* a legacy from one of the most beautiful musical epochs, is moreover marked by no stain of degeneracy. Too often civilisation tends to be confounded with the refinement of luxury shown by the ages of decadence. And lately we have heard a foreign conductor, on reading the Trio of the master, speak of " romantic femininity." Nothing could be more false : it is, on the contrary, classic and virile art. It does not follow that what is sensitive and not barbarian should be affected, or that pure music and sound construction should remain absent.

But precisely because of its qualities, it happens that it is misunderstood. It is quite true that, in France, a more and more numerous *élite* of initiates are forming a sort of " Faurian freemasonry," amongst whom the musical gifts, the taste, and fineness of their harmonic ear are proved, in truth, by this common sympathy. For them, the general incompetency of the critics could be measured by their non-comprehension of Gabriel Fauré : and I for one do not find this claim ridiculous. But in opposition to this select band, even in our own country, is the mass of the uneducated, and particularly—a more serious fact—those music-lovers whose culture is specially due to the art of Beethoven and his successors.[1]  The study of this lack of comprehension rounds off this discussion of Fauré's character.

And first, we do not wish to infer an *a priori* eulogy because his art is French.  We do not praise these qualities because they are ours, but because they seem praiseworthy ; and we can congratulate ourselves that they represent at the same time the pure French tradition, proving that the spirit of our artists, poets and musicians is rooted in things good *in themselves*, and exclusive of all nationalistic vainglory.  But we cannot overlook the fact that elsewhere, perhaps, these things are misunderstood, and that a public for whom Tschaikowsky (with the undesirable Pathetic Symphony) is a great master, has necessarily quite a different conception from ours—and less classic.

Two trends are clearly discernible in the musicians of other countries : the one, a sentimentality (necessarily harmful), emphatic, turgid and cloying all at once ; the other, brutality—often barbarous, but vital (R. Strauss, Hindemith, Prokofiev, etc.).[2]  In contrast to these two tendencies there are respectively :

1st.  The *Logic* of Fauré, because of which the Beethoven fanatics, misled, consider him cold, or at least, " perfect, but with no emotion." We have had occasion to discuss the matter with a music-lover of this sort ; but as (with the assurance of ignorance) he addressed the same reproach to Bach—judging him scholastic—we carried the discussion no farther.  These dullards have blinkers—or rather, earplugs—which render them deaf.  It is probable that such a listener, swooning at the floods of emotion of the Pathetic Symphony, would be insensitive to the 2nd Quintet.  That is regrettable, but what can be done ? And one is reminded of Boubouroche denying his wife's unfaithful nature. . . .

2nd.  His *Sensitiveness*, considered by some, as we have seen, to be " romantic femininity."  Lately, some criticisms from beyond the Rhine have contained denunciations of God knows what " Parisian superficiality."[3]  Some modern theories, analagous to those of Saint-Saëns on the possibility of a " purely plastic "[4] music, would have Form and Expression opposed to each other.[5]  *A priori* this is open to question, and *a posteriori* there is nothing in the history of music to confirm it.  People go to the extent of neglecting the very profound and ever-present sentiment of Bach, clinging to the intellectualism of his " exact form "—whereas his form shows great diversity and his art great expression !  This " revolt against expression " (pedantic rather than new), this neo-classic conception (though there is little

---

[1] *The point requires a little elucidation.  It is principally a matter of* harmonic culture, *more even than the expressive character, or the turns of phrase.  But there is no doubt that the style of Brahms, and even on occasion that of Beethoven, is very different from the styles of Bach, Mozart and Fauré.  It must not be concluded from this that the latter did not understand Beethoven !*

[2] *It is doubtful whether to add Stravinsky, whose sort of inner barbarity is so natural and precise, so lucid and well-turned, that it acquires the qualities of classicism, even apart from the fine transcription of* Pulcinella.

[3] *Always this old nonsense of the French being light, incapable of depth !*

[4] *Cf. the Letters of Saint-Saëns to Camille Bellaigue* (Revue des Deux Mondes).

[5] *People have tried to make an " impressionist " of Claude Debussy, an " expressionist " of Gabriel Fauré.  In which is the* Form *less solid ?*

" classic " about it), this gratuitous, *anti-musical* fashion of separating the expressive element from the constructional factors—all this, it must be realised, is the fashion of the day. Our artists will do well not to let their heads be stuffed with the ideas of the aestheticians. It is obvious that the construction, even the form, can vary with the sentiment, and should do so. We will not labour the point ; the works of Fauré, displaying as perfect a harmony in their balanced design as one could wish, are there for all to see. Clearly, if one banishes love, if one fears all that comes from the heart and ventures only on a sort of " Meccano " construction, one cannot understand his music. But in that case, what true musician could one understand ? And even those who delight in a style of brutal violence, do not they display a sort of expression in reverse ? If their works are living they preserve a relation to human feelings.

There is added a last obstacle, and this not the least one : the language of Gabriel Fauré. More than anything, in the Songs, this habit of expressing himself without insistence perplexes on first hearing ; one has to re-read them and pore over them.[1] But there is also the novelty and subtlety of the syntax.[2] If its elements appear traditional, in reality this music (descending from Gounod and Chopin) differs from Beethoven's. And not only in the general aesthetic (much closer to Bach), nor even in the contrapuntal writing, but above all in the *nature of the harmony ;* it is this, evidently, which perplexes the traditional Beethovenian before a work of Fauré, however great it may be.[3] We have spoken at length of his taste for Plain-song, his Gregorian feelings, his plagal cadences, his very personal modulations. In all these regards he is seen to be infinitely further from those one calls " the classics " than Richard Wagner. Beethoven in his time, and after his fashion, was extremely bold ; a creator of the utmost freedom, as the dismay of many musicians at his first performances in France will testify (cf. Berlioz' *Mémoires*). And it is a very regrettable convention, contrary to the *true Beethoven tradition*—of feeling and independence—not to venture from his principal harmonies ; but the intolerance of the ear is great, and audiences are easily disconcerted. An art as new, in its turn, as Fauré's was received with reserve by Ambroise Thomas just as, even to-day, is done by certain belated critics, unable to see that a warm welcome for the present does not prevent them, if they wish, from holding in permanent affection the beauties of yesterday.

To appreciate at its true value the music of *Pénélope, la Bonne Chanson* or the 2nd Quintet, the ear must be guided along harmonic lines already familiar : usual enough in France—that is, among the elect—since a number of our composers have similar ways of expressing themselves—but much rarer in other countries, where the majority of the public still thinks in the language of yesterday,[4] accepting if

---

[1] *This is why French music, with its reserve and compactness, is more difficult to understand than Wagner.*

[2] *More than the vocabulary.*

[3] *For it is often by the beauty of this harmony that the expression, in his case, is made so intense.*

[4] *With a notable inability to understand any harmonisation derived from Gregorian Modes.*

need be a certain uncouth bitonality, less new at bottom than Fauré's conceptions. In addition, some general culture appears necessary—an *Attic sense* whose value is not appreciated by everybody[1] ; and the understanding that quality outweighs quantity. Finally—and this is perhaps essential—there must be a moral sense ; a leaning towards goodness, seriousness and depth ; never admitting an art merely amusing, or brutal, or vulgarly emphatic.

Considered from this point of view Fauré's art offers a most instructive lesson. It will be not unhelpful to particularise, which we propose to do in these final pages.

From its Greek nature it follows first that this art, sober and temperate, is not overwhelming. Its spaciousness, free from ambition and vanity, is the final goal led up to by song, sonata and quartet (sometimes it has been achieved earlier, almost at the outset of this journey ; cf. *Chant d'automne, Après un Rêve*, the 1876 Violin Sonata, etc.). Nothing is more salutary than to remember that such an artist, despising none of his colleagues, and no technique, however common—with no proud premeditation and almost unconsciously, could produce such great and powerful music ; it should teach us both confidence and modesty. Certainly, his emotional capacity was very great, and the gift is indeed rare which can discover harmony in matter, can ensnare the beauty existing in the world and finally transpose life into terms of art, bequeathing to men the best of himself. Others may be less liberally endowed ; but if they develop the gifts of the good fairies in the best and healthiest conditions, they need not lose heart.

In the first place, the regard for expression, needful at all times, would to-day be the surest antidote to that withering indifference which paralyses inspiration. As for the Fauré *modesty,* and the summits to which it leads the musician, the question is closely connected with the relativity of the force and the artistic grandeur. No need to pile Pelion upon Ossa to reach the Olympians ; and the route to Parnassus is " with a good grace " and simplicity of soul. More true grandeur is to be found in a few clear lines (such as a Bach Chorale, or a Fauré Mélodie : " O Mort, poussière d'étoiles . . .") than in many a long and ambitious symphony, empty and bombastic. A simple hand sketched by da Vinci, a negro study by Rubens, are durable things ; it is of slight importance that the study in question does not deal with a precise subject, or is only a fragment ! Life and beauty are the things which count, not the genre of the work, nor its *apparent* dimensions, nor even that it is " unfinished " : there is but one Act only of *la Briséis*, by Chabrier, or of Mussorgsky's *Mariage*. Mozart's " Exercises in strict counterpoint,"[2] Claude Debussy's or Maurice Ravel's harmony exercises, would be infinitely superior in interest to some mediocre lyric drama or symphony. It will not be contested that there is some *absolute* quality in the power

---

[1] *With which* attention *goes hand in hand ; Fauré's music is not such as one can listen to inattentively.*

[2] *Beethoven's have been published—and very unequal they are (to say the least). He could never conform to this discipline, despite real effort. But the " school studies " of Mozart ought to be charming.*

# Gabriel Fauré

of the orchestra, as in the time-scale. Certain thoughts, certain works, demand a vast canvas; for example, *Prométhée*. But it is clear (and Fauré continually provides the example) that a highly sensitive artist, given the talent to render this sensitivity articulate, requires but a page to achieve a rare beauty. *L'Invitation au voyage* or *l'Élégie* suffice to prove Duparc a great musician. In fact, we come back always to the comparison of the Parthenon with *la Cité* of Carcassonne—or simply, that of a marble fragment, a relic of the Acropolis, with a clock casing in "artistic bronze," or the official and deplorable public statue.

We have already gathered that his compositions originated in a sort of *moral* quality, as much as in what comes from the heart, as in that confidence in an unambitious type of beauty, and in that calm assurance of the relativity of greatness—since the inner life of the music and the manner of its realisation are the only things of importance. The very life-story, the study of Fauré's art, *from the moral point of view*, offers the most profitable object lesson.

"Cultivons notre jardin . . ." Aptitudes and tastes vary, but it is a universal maxim. To realise it you have only to ask yourself this question: How came Fauré ceaselessly to develop, and not squander, the gifts which the Goddess brought to his cradle?

By unremitting work, in the balancing of discipline and freedom. This discipline, dating from l'École Niedermeyer—and also from the excellent lessons he had from Saint-Saëns, fugue and strict counterpoint—this respect for order, to which he submitted, and which he continued to observe of his own free will, that harmonious Reason that he loved, that his artistic nature demanded—such were also the characteristics of the composer of Henry VIII.[1] But the latter included in his intellectual equipment a certain amount of needless science. He reasoned sometimes *a priori;* an argument in general superficial and not rigorous, and positively false, since one is tempted to apply it in all cases. Fauré had the advantage on the contrary, of never wasting his time in that way. He had the wisdom to control his feelings only by his instinct; by the bounds of taste, and not by regrettable hypotheses about "purely plastic" compositions. He had little interest in how a work was labelled, or any of the side issues of art, and particularly whether or no he was writing "pure music." He cared only for music, pure and simple. Then the magic flower blossomed, with its undying perfume.

But Fauré's freedom is more than simply the disdain of useless theories, or than technical daring. It proceeds from moral causes, from the character of the man.[2]

This freedom showed itself independent of the dictates of fashion; having "something to say" he remained free from pushfulness, from commercialism, from histrionics, from all taint of playing to the gallery—whence the most fecund individualism. It is needless to insist on the dangers of fashion, the unhealthy futility of bowing

---

[1] *i.e., Saint-Saëns.*

[2] *And after all, it is always the* man *that we find in the works of an artist* : *we benefit or suffer from the good or bad qualities of his inner being.*

to its decrees.[1] This kind of " novelty " declares itself the very
negation of art—lacking personality, feeling, or creation. To say of
music : this harmony is *démodé*, these accompaniments should be
thrown on the scrap-heap—this is clearly stupid. All durable beauty
is born, lives and survives eternally, *apart from fashion*.[2] The artist
demands an aesthetic diametrically opposed to that of the " man
of the world " whose eye is (temporarily) accustomed to some baroque
line, some illogical proportion, ugly in itself, simply because it is
*chic*. Fauré was neither Wagnerian, nor Franckist, nor Debussyist,
nor Ravelian, nor " Eriksatieist "—nor Stravinskyist. All the movements which influenced the opinions of the snobs, if he did not seek
to flee from them (which would have been a slavery in reverse), at
least he was never shaken by their eddies.[3]

To be oneself : on this condition only, can one show oneself diverse,
profound, and true.

But *individualism* has sometimes a bad press. It will be objected :
" If the composer shows himself individual, living in his own thoughts,
dreaming only of what *he* finds in the poets, in nature, and in the events
of his own life—if he neglects to this degree the surrounding feeling,
he will not be truly representative, he will have no existence for the
crowd." And this means discussing the question of popular music.
But first, what is this " surrounding feeling " ? If one considers it
in its less elevated—and most customary—aspect, it is only a question
of the art of the populace, of unpleasant demagogy. Why may the
artist not be aristocratic ? Why indeed, *should* he not be, if you
take the word in its original connotation, derived from " the best " ?
" Enough of *learned music*, made for an *élite* of *Mandarins* ! "
What a dangerous thesis ! Must there not, always, be some development of the musical sense, acquired by repeated hearings ? Without
a little culture to start with, would you understand Beethoven's
Fourteenth Quartet ? This has been necessary for us, the professionals[4] ; by what privilege is the rest of society exempt ? Moreover,
the experience of all high inspiration demands a different culture :
not specially literary, but rather general and, ultimately, *moral*. Thus

---

[1]*This does not mean that, in certain exceptionally privileged epochs, the best art
cannot be in agreement with official and national fashions—a general style, a universal
feeling. This is to be seen in the time of Pericles. But the citizens of Athens formed
an aristocracy ; and even then it is not certain that each artist did not preserve his own
idiosyncrasies, and sometimes (as with Euripedes) a cast of mind hardly satisfactory
to the opinion of the majority.*

[2]*Or at least, if it is found to be in agreement with the fashion, this is a coincidence,
and not obedience on the part of the artist.*

[3]*It is of the first importance to recall that Fauré never ceased to be faithful to those
he admired, and that the disparagements of cliques had no effect on him. At the time
of the Wagner idolatry, when it was the height of fashion to despise Gounod, Fauré took
care never to change his opinion of* Venise *and the Duo from* Faust. *More recently,
when a " triple alliance" of the Schola Cantorum, a number of Debussy's followers
(but not including Ravel !), and some of the polytonalists, were battering down Saint-
Saëns' reputation—an excess of censure after a glory perhaps too effulgent—the old
pupil of l'École Niedermeyer was not only proclaiming that he owed everything to the
composer of the charming and little known* Ascanio, *but even maintaining that, in his
opinion, this musician was one of the foremost of the French School.*

[4]*And even before the study of technique, of which there is here no question ; the
culture referred to is the knowledge of and insight into the works.*

—after a little acclimatising in these works—we see people whose musical education has been quite negligible enthusing over *Pénélope*, and *Pelléas et Mélisande*, by reason of their own sensitivity, and thanks to the *quality* of a sufficiently developed " inner being." Conversely, some vulgar souls, despite their natural aptitude for the art of sounds, will never understand,—music, except by a miracle, and momentarily, never lifts them above their level, or awakens in them anything of nobility. But they would never be converted by means of the mediocre. However, what is the meaning of this vague term, " learned music " ? It is used to describe an elevated, contrapuntal style—that is to say, writing in several parts, with harmony not absolutely elementary. Some would wish to see it banished.[1] Happily, an experience of Albert-Doyen, with the *Mastersingers* at the *Fêtes du Peuple*, was conclusive. The polyphony of the third Act discouraged none of the participators—all very modest in technique.[2] The Bach Chorales met with a like success. It is probable that some scenes from *Prométhée* would succeed no less[3] ; Fauré's art, personal though it may be, reveals itself as universal, and even popular—in the best sense of the word. But it is necessary to educate the people up to it. And no slogan of " art for all " will excuse concessions to the " *vulgum pecus.*"

At bottom, it seems that the objections to individualism spring from a confusion of words. The artist—" collective " or not—is necessarily an individual. His *métier*, his imagination, his feeling are his own ; the truer he remains to himself, the more living, enduring and human he is, and the further, in the long run, will his work spread. Paradox, if you will ; but an incontestable truth proved by the actual history of music.

It is a curious thing, that in the " simple soul " of Gabriel Fauré should be found a certain affinity with young people, though his sensitivity seems quite different. To become a child again, or never to lose one's childlike simplicity of character, that one may love certain chords, and *dare* to write them—some newcomers have understood the worth of this quality. Chabrier reveals it, in *la Bourrée Fantasque*, and Fauré very often. Do not think that this is antagonistic to forceful maturity ; it only makes it sincere and strong. For *Prométhée* in its prerequisite ingenuousness has nothing of a false rusticity or manufactured archaism, of elemental demagogy or fictitious power. It is to be sincerely hoped that the generations to come will be able to profit by this lesson. The great musicians, the Faurés, Debussys and Stravinskys, are *themselves*. If it is not wise to shun *a priori* the " impressionism "[4] of Debussy—i.e., an art

[1] *But then, the Beethoven Quartets would have to be included in this banishment ! And it is not clear why Fauré's* Prométhée, *or his Second Quintet, would be any more* mandarin-*like than the Andantes of either the 16th or 15th Quartets.*

[2] *The choral part was sung by heart. We would not say that the public grasped straight away all the beauties of this work ; but they were not absolutely against it. And gradually, by helpful repetitions, they came to understand the music.*

[3] *The first Act, for example. Remember, too, that it was sung by Bitterois amateurs.*

[4] *With all reserve concerning the legitimacy of this word as applied to Debussy— and remembering that the composer of* Pelléas, *when he liked, could show himself powerful, even violent.*

of soft and pleasing values—in the hope (sometimes vain) of being strong ; if, as always, it is a snare to yield to fashion (that of to-day being to extol raucous sounds)[1], it is another thing to be hypnotised by the *distinction* of the Debussyan and Verlainian melancholy,[2] in the fear of all homely expression, in order to achieve a certain degeneracy (the fashion of yesterday), in point of fact far removed from Debussy.

This hankering after distinction, under the influence of *Pelléas* and *l'Heure espagnole*, has its dangers. But on the other hand it is both vain and weak to turn one's back on Debussy. Now Fauré's example, *morally* speaking, is much healthier, because, being master of himself, he had the strength to shun violent changes ; because he despised no art ; because he strove to recognise the beautiful in all its forms.

" Pure music." There can be no question about that. But why is this " musicality " beautiful ? And what is the lesson ? Not to imitate him. For are there any chords or progressions that one could class *a priori* as ugly or beautiful ? (Nevertheless, in the plastic arts, running shorts, or a moustache cut " *à la americaine*," are ugly, and the robe of the huntress Diana beautiful ; but there is here the intervention of the proportions of the whole, a human logic—and even of sensitiveness, because of expression resulting from lines more or less felicitous.) In music, would it be sufficient to adopt certain well known progressions *à la* Fauré, to achieve a Faurian beauty, or simply, *Beauty* ? Not at all ; and what traps one would fall into ! Quite definitely, it seems to us that *good sounding harmony* corresponds to the Greek perfection, to a certain serenity of soul. But there is also the dramatic impetus ; *sometimes* this demands other progressions, unexpected asperities. And then, in some instances, there is a mingling of sentiments apparently opposed to each other ; the two kinds of harmonisation can be combined—in what proportion will depend on the individual case. Romanticism assimilated, put in order, overcome and mastered, becomes a source of riches : art becomes then transformed into a broad and new classicism ; it is seen in the case of Gabriel Fauré. On the other hand, the artificial, catalogued, formalised serenity is no more than lifeless academicism—false and stereotyped classicism. There is no recipe for Fauré's art, for none would prove itself sufficiently supple ; and one could use his progressions to advantage only if one already possessed, in a kindred form, something of his own beauty in the sentiments expressed : it would then be coincidental, as with the Tritone in Marguerite's air (from *Faust*) and the harmonies we admire so much in the *Sérénade toscane* or *le Lamento*.

In conclusion, it is then the *moral* teaching of his work, his life, his being—as we have just defined it—which is the beacon for the younger generation, if they will only make up their minds to be guided by it ; and with this wish we close the volume. There lies

[1] *In contrast, mark the harmonious forcefulness of* Prométhée.

[2] *Already, in Wagner's time, the supporters of complex " alterations " displayed a most unmusical and limitless contempt for Gounod. Always Fashion and its evils—and always Pride, " the deadliest of human counsellors ! "*

the road of art—in charm, purity, and strength of writing—in seriousness and depth of feeling—in the natural, honest conscience and the
high ideals of an individualism which yielded to no concession—
such is his lesson. Already some of his qualities have ceased to be
misunderstood by the younger generation ; their successors, if they
will reject the influence of Operetta and the clamour of the market-
place, will be able to comprehend him to the full as a " *gloire classique* "
of France : " the greatest living musician " wrote Gaston Carraud
just before his death. But is he not still living, will he not live for
ever, while men are capable of the love of Music ?

# List of Works

This list is based on that published during Fauré's lifetime in *la Revue Musicale*, Oct., 1922. Some emendations and corrections have been suggested in the course of the work ; thus, the songs of the first volume probably extend over a fairly long period, somewhere around 1865. With regard to the first Quintet, it is very probable that the opening Allegro corresponds to the work announced as Op. 60, and also that the rest of Op. 89 was finished well before 1906, the date of its publication. Finally, *Prison* and *Soir* formerly were numbered Op. 73 and not 83, their composition and even the date of publication being, to all appearances, anterior to that given in the official list (1900).

Many of the songs being published in different keys, it has been thought useful to indicate what was the original key ; this has been inserted, in brackets, after the title, where necessary.

| Opus No. | Title. | Date. | Publisher. |
|---|---|---|---|
| 1 ⌠Le Papillon et la fleur (Victor Hugo) .. | About 1865 | Hamelle |
| ⌡Mai (V. Hugo) .. .. .. .. | ,, | ,, |
| 2 ⌠Dans les ruines d'une abbaye (V. Hugo) .. | ,, | ,, |
| ⌡Les Matelots (Théophile Gautier) .. .. | ,, | ,, |
| 3 ⌠Seule (Th. Gautier) .. .. .. .. | ,, | ,, |
| ⌡Sérénade toscane (Romain Bussine) .. | ,, | ,, |
| 4 ⌠Chanson du pêcheur (Th. Gautier) .. | ,, | ,, |
| ⌡Lydia (Leconte de Lisle) .. .. .. | ,, | ,, |
| 5 ⌠Chant d'automne (Charles Baudelaire) .. | ,, | ,, |
| ⌡Rêve d'amour (V. Hugo) .. .. .. | ,, | ,, |
| ⌞L'Absent (V. Hugo) .. .. .. | ,, | ,, |
| 6 ⌠Aubade (L. Pomey) .. .. .. | ,, | ,, |
| ⌡Tristesse (Th. Gautier) .. .. .. | ,, | ,, |
| 7 ⌠Sylvie (P. de Choudens) .. .. .. | ,, | ,, |
| ⌡Après un rêve (R. Bussine) .. .. | ,, | ,, |
| ⌡Hymne (Baudelaire) .. .. .. | ,, | ,, |
| ⌞Barcarolle (Marc Monnier) .. .. | ,, | ,, |
| 8 ⌠Au bord de l'eau (Sully-Prudhomme) .. | ,, | ,, |
| ⌡La Rançon (Baudelaire) .. .. .. | ,, | ,, |
| ⌞Ici-bas (Sully-Prudhomme) .. .. .. | ,, | ,, |
| 9 | | |
| 10 ⌠" Puisqu'ici-bas (V. Hugo) (duet for two Sopranos) .. .. .. .. .. | About 1870 | ,, |
| ⌡Tarentelle (M. Monnier) (duet for two Sopranos) .. .. .. .. .. | ,, | ,, |
| 11 Cantique de Racine (Chorus, mixed voices, with accpt. for harmonium and str. quintet) .. .. .. .. .. | About 1873 | ,, |
| 12 Les Djinns (V. Hugo) (Chorus for mixed voices, with orchestral accpt.) .. .. | About 1875 | ,, |
| (The actual dates of these two compositions were much earlier.) | | |
| 13 Sonata, in A, for piano and violin.. .. | 1876 | Breitkopf & Härtel |
| 14 Concerto for Violin and Orchestra .. | 1878 | Unpublished |
| 15 1st Quartet (C. Minor), piano and strings | 1879 | Hamelle |

| Opus No. | Title. | Date. | Publisher. |
|---|---|---|---|
| 16 | Berceuse, for piano and violin .. .. | 1880 | Hamelle |
| 17 | 3 Romances without words, for piano solo | 1883 | ,, |
| 18 | Nell (Leconte de Lisle) (G flat) .. .. | About 1880 | ,, |
|  | Le Voyageur (Armand Silvestre) (F min.) | ,, | ,, |
|  | Automne (A. Silvestre) (B min.) .. .. | ,, | ,, |
| 19 | Ballade, for piano and orchestra (originally for piano solo) .. .. .. .. | 1881 | ,, |
| 20 | Suite, for orchestra .. .. .. .. | 1875 | Unpublished except for first movement— see Op. 68 |
| 21 | Poème d'un jour (Ch. Grandmougin) .. | 1881 | Durand |
|  | Rencontre (E maj.) |  |  |
|  | Toujours (E min.) |  |  |
|  | Adieu (E maj.) |  |  |
| 22 | Le Ruisseau, chorus for female voices .. | — | Hamelle |
| 23 | Les Berceaux (Sully-Prudhomme) (B flat min.) | 1882 | ,, |
|  | Notre Amour (A. Silvestre) (E maj.) .. | ,, | ,, |
|  | Le Secret (A. Silvestre) (D min.) .. .. | ,, | ,, |
| 24 | Elegy, for piano and violoncello .. .. | 1883 | ,, |
| 25 | 1st Impromptu, for piano solo (E flat) .. | ,, | ,, |
| 26 | 1st Barcarolle, for piano solo (A min.) .. | ,, | ,, |
| 27 | Chanson d'amour (A. Silvestre) (F maj.) .. | ,, | ,, |
|  | La Fée aux Chansons (A. Silvestre) (F maj.) | ,, | ,, |
| 28 | Romance (B flat), for violin and orchestra | 1882 | ,, |
| 29 | La Naissance de Vénus (P. Collin), mythological scene for soli, chorus and orchestra .. .. .. .. | ,, | ,, |
| 30 | 1st Valse-Caprice (A), for piano solo .. | 1883 | ,, |
| 31 | 2nd Impromptu (F min.), for piano solo .. | ,, | ,, |
| 32 | Mazurka, for piano solo .. .. .. | ,, | ,, |
| 33 | Three Nocturnes (E flat min., B, A flat), for piano solo .. .. .. .. | ,, | ,, |
| 34 | 3rd Impromptu, (A flat) for piano solo .. | ,, | ,, |
| 35 | Madrigal (A. Silvestre), vocal quartet (or chorus) and orchestra .. .. .. | 1884 | ,, |
| 36 | 4th Nocturne (E flat), for piano solo .. | ,, | ,, |
| 37 | 5th Nocturne (B flat), for piano solo .. | ,, | ,, |
| 38 | 2nd Valse-Caprice (D flat), for piano solo.. | ,, | ,, |
| 39 | Aurore (A. Silvestre), (G maj.) .. .. | ,, | ,, |
|  | Fleur jetée (A. Silvestre) (F min.) .. |  |  |
|  | Le Pays des rêves (A. Silvestre) (A flat) .. |  |  |
|  | Les Roses d'Ispahan (Leconte de Lisle) .. |  |  |
| 40 | Symphony in D minor .. .. .. | ,, | Unpublished |
| 41 | 2nd Barcarolle (G maj.), for piano solo .. | 1885 | Hamelle |
| 42 | 3rd Barcarolle (G flat), for piano solo .. | ,, | ,, |
| 43 | Noël (Victor Wilder) .. .. .. | 1886 | ,, |
| 44 | 4th Barcarolle (A flat), for piano solo .. | ,, | ,, |
| 45 | 2nd Quartet (G min.), for piano and strings | ,, | ,, |
| 46 | Les Présents (Villiers de l'Isle-Adam) (F maj.) | 1887 | ,, |
|  | Clair de lune (Paul Verlaine) (B flat min.) | ,, | ,, |
| 47 | O Salutaris, solo .. .. .. .. | About 1887 | ,, |
|  | Maria, mater gratiae, duet .. .. .. | ,, | ,, |
| 48 | Requiem Mass, for soli, chorus, organ and orchestra .. .. .. .. .. | 1887–88 | ,, |

| | | Date. | Publisher. |
|---|---|---|---|
| | | bout 1887 | Unpublished |
| | | 1887 | Hamelle |
| | | bout 1889 | ,, |
| | | ,, | ,, |
| | | ,, | ,, |
| | | ,, | ,, |
| | | Nov. 1888 (Odéon) | ,, |
| | | bout 1890 | ,, |
| | | ,, | ,, |
| | | 893–96 | Hamelle (1st edn. Metzler & Co., London) |
| | | 'th Dec. 1889 (Odéon) | Hamelle |

| 58 | Five songs, the so-called " Venice " songs, to words by Verlaine .. .. .. Mandoline (G) ; En sourdine (E flat) ; Green (G flat) C'est l'extase (D min.) ; A Clymène (E min.) | 1890 | ,, |
| 59 | 3rd Valse-Caprice (G flat), for piano solo | 1891 | ,, |
| 60 | Quintet, announced under this No. (see Op. 89) .. .. .. .. .. | ,, | ,, |
| 61 | La Bonne Chanson (Verlaine) Song cycle.. (Une sainte en son auréole ; Puisque l'aube grandit ; La Lune blanche ; J'allais par des chemins perfides ; J'ai presque peur, en verité ; Avant que tu ne t'en ailles ; Donc, ce sera par un clair jour d'été ; N'est-ce pas ? ; L'Hiver a cessé) .. | 1891–92 | ,, |
| 62 | 4th Valse-Caprice (A flat), for piano solo.. | About 1894 | ,, |
| 63 | 6th Nocturne (D flat), for piano solo .. | ,, | ,, |
| 63 | Hymn to Apollo, Greek Chant of 11th Century B.C., discovered at Delphos by the French School of Athens. Greek text reconstituted by H. Weil. Transcribed by Th. Reinach. Accpt. by Gabriel Fauré .. .. .. .. | 1894 | S. Borneman (Published also by Novello) |
| 64 | | | |
| 65 | Ave Verum, duet (or chorus) for female voices .. .. .. .. | About 1894 | Hamelle |
| | Tantum ergo, Chorus for three female voices with soli .. .. .. .. .. | ,, | ,, |
| 66 | 5th Barcarolle (F sharp min.), for piano solo | About 1895 | ,, |
| 67 | Salve Regina, solo .. .. .. .. | About 1895 | Hamelle |
| | Ave Maria, solo .. ... .. .. | ,, | ,, |
| 68 | Allegro symphonique (first movement of Op. 20), for orchestra .. .. .. | 1875 | ,, |
| 69 | Romance in A, for violoncello and piano.. | About 1895 | ,, |
| 70 | 6th Barcarolle (E flat), for piano solo .. | About 1896 | ,, |

| Opus No. | Title. | Date. | Publisher. |
|---|---|---|---|
| 95 | La Chanson d'Ève (Van Lerberghe), Song cycle (Paradis ; Prima verba ; Roses ardentes ; Comme Dieu rayonne ; L'aube blanche ; Eau vivante ; Veilles-tu, ma senteur de soleil ? ; D'un parfum de roses blanches ; Crépuscule ; O Mort, poussière d'étoiles) .. .. .. | 1907–10 | Heugel |
| 96 | 8th Barcarolle (D min.), for piano solo .. | 1908 | ,, |
| 97 | 9th Nocturne (B min.), for piano solo .. | ,, | ,, |
| 98 | Serenade, for violoncello and piano .. | ,, | ,, |
| 99 | 10th Nocturne (E min.), for piano solo .. | 1909 | ,, |
| 100 | — | | |
| 101 | 9th Barcarolle (A min.), for piano solo .. | 1910 | ,, |
| 102 | 5th Impromptu (F sharp min.) .. .. | ,, | ,, |
| 103 | 9 Preludes, for piano solo (in D flat, C min., G min., F, D min., E flat min., A, C min., and E min.) ... .. .. .. .. | 1910–11 | ,, |
| 104 | 11th Nocturne (G min.), and 10th Barcarolle (A min.), for piano solo .. .. .. | 1913 | Durand |
| 105 | 11th and 12th Barcarolles (G min., E flat), for piano solo .. .. .. .. | 1914–16 | ,, |
| 106 | Le Jardin clos (Van Lerberghe), Song cycle (Exaucement ; Quand tu plonges tes yeux dans mes yeux ; La Messagère ; Je me poserai sur ton coeur ; Dans la nymphée ; Dans la pénombre ; Il m'est cher, amour ; Inscription sur le sable) .. .. .. .. .. | 1915(?)–18 | ,, |
| 107 | 12th Nocturne (E min.), for piano solo .. | 1916 | ,, |
| 108 | 2nd Sonata (E min.), for violin and piano | 1917 | ,, |
| 109 | 1st Sonata (D min.), for violoncello and piano .. .. .. .. .. | 1918 | ,, |
| 110 | " Une chatelaine en sa tour," for harp solo | ,, | ,, |
| 111 | Fantaisie (G maj.), for piano and orchestra | 1919 | ,, |
| 112 | Masques et Bergamasques, Suite for orchestra .. .. .. .. .. | 1920 | ,, |
| 113 | Mirages (Baronne de Brimont), song cycle ; (Cygne sur l'eau ; Reflets dans l'eau ; Jardin nocturne ; Danseuse) .. .. | 1919 | ,, |
| 114 | C'est la paix (Mlle. Georgette Dubladis) .. | 1919–20 | ,, |
| 115 | 2nd Quintet, for piano and strings.. .. | 1921 | ,, ✓ |
| 116 | 13th Barcarolle (C maj.), for piano solo .. | ,, | ,, |
| 117 | 2nd Sonata, for violoncello and piano (G min.) .. .. .. .. .. | 1922 | ,, |
| 118 | L'Horizon chimérique (Jean de la Ville de Mirmont), Song cycle. (La Mer est infinie ; Je me suis embarqué ; Diane, Séléné ; Vaisseaux, nous vous aurons aimés) .. .. .. .. .. | ,, | ,, |
| 119 | 13th Nocturne (B min.), for piano solo .. | ,, | ,, |
| 120 | Trio, for piano, violin and violoncello .. | 1923 | ,, |
| 121 | String quartet .. .. .. .. | 1924 | ,, |

## Works without Opus numbers :

| | | |
|---|---|---|
| En prière (Stephane Bordèse) .. .. | 1890 | Durand |
| Le Ramier (A. Silvestre) .. .. .. | 1904 | Hamelle |
| Vocalise (in vol. 1 of a collection of vocalises by M. Hettich) .. .. .. .. | 1907 | Leduc |
| Tantum ergo, for soprano or tenor and mixed voices .. .. .. .. | 1905 | Durand |
| Tantum ergo, for mezzo-soprano or baritone, with unison chorus *ad libitum* .. | 1905 | Durand |
| Tu es Petrus, for baritone solo and mixed voices .. .. .. .. .. | 1884 | ,, |
| Low mass, for three female voices and organ accpt. .. .. .. .. | 1907 (date of publication) | Heugel |
| Pénélope, lyric drama in 3 Acts .. .. | 1913 | Heugel |

# Bibliography

L. Aguettant, " G. Fauré " (Lyons, 1924—no publisher given).
„ " La génie de Gabriel Fauré (Lyons, " Aux deux collines," 1924).
C. Bellaigue, " Études musicales " (3rd Series) (Delagrave, 1907).
Camille Benoit, " Le Requiem de Gabriel Fauré " (Schott and Co., 1888).
A. Bruneau, " La musique française " (Fasquelle, 1901).
„ " Notice sur la vie et les oeuvres de G. Fauré " (read before the Institute, March 28th, 1925).
V. d'Indy, " Cours de composition musicale," 2nd volume (Durand).
Ch. Koechlin, contributions to " l'Encyclopédie de la musique " (Delagrave). 2nd part, vol. 1 (a) Les tendances de la musique française contemporaine ; (b) Étude sur l'harmonie moderne.
J. de Marliave, " Études musicales " (F. Alcan).
H. Riemann, " Dictionnaire de musique," translated and revised by G. Humbert (Perrin, 1899).
Oct. Séré, " Musiciens d'aujourd'hui " (Mercure de France, 1911).
Ed. Schuré, " Profils de musiciens."
L. Vuillemin, " G. Fauré, sa vie et son oeuvre," (Durand).
E. Vuillermoz, " Musiques d'aujourd'hui " (C. Crès, 1923).
" Cinquante années de musique française (Librairie de France, 1924–26) ; articles by L. Laloy, H. Malherbe, E. Vuillermoz, Ch. Koechlin, P. Hermant, A. Coeuroy).
Special number of " la Revue musicale," Oct. 1922.

Books, periodicals, etc. not listed by Koechlin.

(a) French books :—
Vladimir Jankélévitch, " Gabriel Fauré et ses mélodies " (Librairie Plon, Paris).
Philippe Fauré-Frémiet, " Gabriel Fauré " (Paris).
(These two have been published since Koechlin's " Fauré ").
A. Cortot, " French piano music (O.U.P., 1932, translated by Hilda Andrews).
André Coeuroy, " La Musique francaise moderne " (Librairie Delagrave, 1922).
G. Jean-Aubrey, " French music of to-day " (Kegan Paul, 1919, translated by Edwin Evans).
(b) English reference books and periodicals ;—
W. W. Cobbett, " Cyclopedic Survey of Chamber Music " (O.U.P., 1929–30— brief summaries of most of the chamber works).
Grove's Dictionary of Music (Macmillan).
Aaron Copland, " Gabriel Fauré, a neglected master," article in the " Musical Quarterly," Oct., 1924.
M. D. Calvocoressi, obituary notice in " Musical Times," Dec., 1924.
Florent Schmitt, obituary notice in the " Chesterian," Dec., 1924.
Leslie Orrey, two articles on " the songs " and " the chamber music," " Musical Opinion," April–May, 1945.
Leslie Orrey, " Gabriel Fauré, 1845–1924," " Musical Times," May, 1945.
„ „ " The songs of Gabriel Fauré," " The Music Review," May, 1945.
Norman Suckling, " The songs of Fauré," " The Listener," Mar. 15th, 1945.
„ „ " Gabriel Fauré, Classic of Modern Times," " The Music Review," May, 1945.
Norman Suckling, " The Unknown Fauré," " Monthly Musical Record," May, 1945.
Martin Cooper, " Some Aspects of Fauré's Technique," " Monthly Musical Record," May, 1945.
Edward Lockspeiser, " Fauré and the Song," " Monthly Musical Record," May, 1945.

# INDEX